SUN STIGMATA
(SCULPTURE POEMS)

PREVIOUSLY BY EILEEN R. TABIOS

POETRY
After The Egyptians Determined The Shape of the World is a Circle, 1996
Beyond Life Sentences, 1998
The Empty Flagpole (CD with guest artist Mei-mei Berssenbrugge), 2000
Ecstatic Mutations, 2001 (with short stories and essays)
Reproductions of The Empty Flagpole, 2002
Enheduanna in the 21st Century, 2002
There, Where the Pages Would End, 2003
Menage a Trois With the 21st Century, 2004
Crucial Bliss Epilogues, 2004
The Estrus Gaze(s), 2005
SONGS OF THE COLON, 2005
POST BLING BLING, 2005
I Take Thee, English, For My Beloved, 2005
The Secret Lives of Punctuations, Vol. I, 2006
Dredging for Atlantis, 2006
It's Curtains, 2006
SILENCES: The Autobiography of Loss, 2007
The Singer and Others: Flamenco Hay(na)ku, 2007
The Light Sang As It Left Your Eyes: Our Autobiography, 2007
NOTA BENE EISWEIN, 2009
Footnotes to Algebra: Uncollected Poems 1995-2009, 2009
Roman Holiday, 2010
THE THORN ROSARY: Selected Prose Poems and New 1998-2010, 2010
the relational elations   of ORPHANED ALGEBRA (with j/j hastain), 2012
5 Shades of Gray, 2012
THE AWAKENING: A Long Poem Triptych & A Poetics Fragment, 2013
147 MILLION ORPHANS (MMXI-MML), 2014
44 RESURRECTIONS, 2014

FICTION
Behind The Blue Canvas, 2004
SILK EGG: Collected Novels 2009-2009, 2011

PROSE COLLECTIONS
Black Lightning, 1998 (poetry essays/interviews)
My Romance, 2002 (art essays with poems)
The Blind Chatelaine's Keys, 2008 (biography with haybun)

SUN STIGMATA
(SCULPTURE POEMS)

For Freline

EILEEN R. TABIOS

MARSH HAWK PRESS, 2014

ISBN (hardcover): 978-0-9882356-6-3
ISBN (paperback): 978-0-9882356-7-0

14 15 16 17 18   7 6 5 4 3 2 1   FIRST EDITION

Marsh Hawk Press books are published by Poetry Mailing List, Inc., a not-for-profit corporation under section 501 (c) 3 of the United States Internal Revenue Code.

Cover Image: Detail from "Marginalia" (2005) by Emmy Catedral, exhibited in "Geography of Now," Pancake Studio, New York, N.Y. (2005)

Book Design: Michelle Bautista

Library of Congress Cataloging-in-Publication Data

Tabios, Eileen.
  [Poems. Selections]
  Sun stigmata : (sculpture poems) / Eileen R. Tabios. -- First edition.
     134 pages ; cm
  ISBN 978-0-9882356-6-3 (hardcover) -- ISBN 0-9882356-6-8 (hardcover) --
  ISBN 978-0-9882356-7-0 (softcover) -- ISBN 0-9882356-7-6 (softcover)
  I. Title.
  PS3570.A234A6 2014
  811'.54--dc23
                      2014032199

Marsh Hawk Press
P.O. Box 206, East Rockaway, N.Y. 11518-0206
mheditor@marshhawkpress.org

Publication of this book was supported by a generous grant from the Council of Literary Magazines and Presses via the New York State Council on the Arts.

Marsh Hawk Press
www.marshhawkpress.org

Dedicated to **Thomas Fink**—poet,
artist, editor, critic, scholar and loyal friend—whose support
led to *Reproductions of the Empty Flagpole*,
my first poetry book publication in the United States.
Tom, *Agyamanac unay.*

CONTENTS

I. REPRODUCTIONS OF THE LOST FLAG:
STIGMATA SCULPTURES

I.
REPRODUCTIONS OF THE LOST FLAG:
STIGMATA SCULPTURES

PREFACE

Stigmata's Poems

> *"Every block of stone has a statue inside it and it is the task of the sculptor to discover it."*
> **—Michelangelo**

What if the block of stone was a block of prose?

These poems were written-sculpted out of the poems of similar titles in the first two sections of my first U.S.-published book and 2002 prose poem collection, *Reproductions of the Empty Flagpole*. I did not sculpt poems from the book's third and last section as those poems were previously wrought from sculptor Anne Truitt's three ravishing and inspirational memoirs.

While sculpting the poems, I was also inspired by an observation—something I've discovered to be a truism even as remains a mystery:

> *"Art: … The prayer that leads to stigmata …"*
> **—Eric Gamalinda**

Also, while I've been prolific in releasing poetry collections, I've always been interested in creating books that are different from each other. I did not want any of my books to predict what might come next. As it turns out, this has meant that in reading older work, I often do not recognize who then was the poet who wrote those poems, the poet behind the persona lurking within the poem(s) and book(s). I used this project as a means to excavate experimentally the author of *Reproductions of the Empty Flagpole*. While each poem can stand on its own, the arc that poems create together to become a poetry collection also create a persona. I wanted to meet this person(a) again as my memory has become murky on hir identity.

Well, I sense that this self was intimate with stigmata—while I don't judge that person for hir predilections, I certainly wouldn't want to wallow in the wound even if it's quite generous as a Muse. When it comes to poetry, I don't want to know myself as a fixed identity. When it comes to poetry, I wish to discover and, at times, change. For, as a poet once said—and this was a poetics statement I discovered as a newbie poet which significantly affected my subsequent development in poetry—

> *Being a poet is not writing a poem but finding a new way to live.*
> **—Paul Le Cour**

I am content with writing—then departing from—these poems derived through stigmata. I opt for a different way to exist, a fresh way to write, a new way to live.

—Eileen R. Tabios

MY GREECE

When a term like symmetria *is used by a late antique rhetorician, one should probably not expect it to have the rigorous precision of meaning that it conveyed to a sculptor of the fifth century B.C. In general, it may be expected that the technical value of a particular term—that is, the value which is dependent upon the special knowledge and training of a particular group—will diminish as the size of the group using the term increases*

—from "The Ancient View of Greek Art" by J.J. Pollitt

(ECLIPSE

Holes in maps look through to nowhere
—Laura Riding Jackson

                ... fled

to an alien land
whose history has become
like you—impossible to be grasped

...to feel the white-haired woman
I will become
(looking through a window and seeing glass)

I never entered a dark building
fraught upon the high heels you love
          feeling the embrace of leers

          a ripped hole in space
                    where I felt you sculpting
                    a dispassionate embrace

How has she become
a shadow when there is no light

(THE KRITIOS BOY

The (in)famous artist
Anonymous
with faint but meticulous scratches

depicts locked eyes
between Achilles and
the Amazon queen Penthiselea
as his sword penetrates her breast—

      unsure with metaphors:

critics and historians hail
"The Kritios Boy"
for immortalizing *hesitation*

Preserve illusion
with a polite silence

No consolation
in memories
that make one catch one's breath

not since a well-intended gesture
eliminated lyrical eyelet lace
from a hand-me-down dress
to create something new for

 a toddler blissful in her ignorance

(PURITY

feeling a deer
quicken its leaps—

      the artist avoided
      aftermaths of wounds

How might a grid eliminate
gesture from paint

viscous as it flows
like a menstruation—

a loss that teaches
the intensity
      of aborted hopes

and failed mitigation
through geometry

Encaustic *will* fail:

did the Greeks attain
Purity?

Did I earn the moments
I made my mother cry

(TO BE SEEN BY IAMOS, CALCHAS AND TEIRESIAS

He carves works that will immortalize
his name as "Anonymous"—

stone shrinks as the sage
peruses a sabotage

I was a fetal heap crumpled
against the other side of your door

Only statues can manifest
what moves me, *moves me*

Your broken bodies manifest
spaces between

signifying this world's only
certainty: *Uncertainty*

Hippodameia today: incom
-plete with feet long gone

broken off at the ankles
prideful crack rising from

right eye to hairline
a missing left arm

She is raising her veil
against my gaze—

the beholder a reflection
she fears—Archaic Greece

feared chaos. Yet again
I look behind me

surreptitiously, in the way
of faux sages throughout history

(ETHOS

missing the tip
    of her nose

slanted cheekbones behind fur

she stiffens my spine into leaving the bed we've never shared

photograph of *Athena, 400 B.C.*

ancient marble reaches across centuries to contradict our people:
    "the Ideal cannot be manifested"

Honor the lucidity of certain objects: *feather diamond rose*
    and others now fallen through the sieve my memory has fought
    against becoming

Once, you hovered—
you desired this knowledge:
    How long can idealism be maintained?

RETURNING THE BORROWED TONGUE

The,hands,on,the,piano,are,armless,
—José García Villa

In 1898, the United States claimed it owned the Philippines after buying it for $20 million from Spain through the Treaty of Paris. The Filipinos—who had won and declared their independence from Spain—protested, and thus commenced the Philippine-American War, a war that has been called the United States' "First Vietnam." With their prowess on the military terrain, the United States defeated the Philippines. The United States solidified its colonialism through the cultural and linguistic terrain with the popularization of English as the preferred language for education, administration, commerce and daily living. Thus, English is sometimes called by Filipinos to be "the borrowed tongue," though "enforced tongue" would be more accurate.

(JADE

…misinterpreted the fall of night
      Against a Grecian urn, shadows sunder
           and are sundered before time's passage

…so difficult to find innocence in accomplished men
      There is always something to be paid

…favorite stone is jade for the impassivity of its face—
      despite charisma
           factually an optical illusion that is solid

O grit of time's encroachment! No need to turn the urn
      to realize I no longer believe
           in the humility of monks

(THE CHASE

You feel
your brow
compress
to sutures

as you
consider
the limpid
light. The

edges of
your vision
shimmers mar-
gins of gold

Once, you
inhaled dust
from a forgot
-ten ciudad

When he
smiled, he
blinded you
with teeth—
you blinked

As lashes
fluttered open
you gleaned
a trail
of smoke

evaporating
from a
cup of tea
suddenly
in your hand

*"Mama, how
did you come
to speak
like this?"*

Chiffon dresses
once swayed
with the breeze
She paused

24

turned to
offer you
an orange
You will
always remember

the experience
of peeling
away thick
hide—jagged

remnants cling-
ing to nails
and skin

"Discuss how
the tilt of
a clock's
minute hand
is both fraught
with meaning
and inconsequential"

These memories
form a single
weight—you
are the one

offering an
extended palm
open and
trusting the
fall of light

against flesh
surrounding
your life lines

Air spills—
your gaze
follows, sees
footsteps

conscientious
-ly straddling
the thinned
excuse for
a rope

(COME KNOCKING

I said, *I love the flag*

You let a sound from the embattled
      street intrude for diversion

But as I turned away
I felt you raise your hand
before it sadly lapsed

 …admired encaustic
for protecting
the fragility of paper

…arms grew wiry tugging at rope
That evening, welts rose—
soothed them with
the wet walls of a beer bottle

What is the surface of reality?

With what are we grappling
when we are dreaming?

How difficult it must be for you—
still, I must come knocking…

(AFTER 2 A.M.

Rain slid like a sheet
Sometimes love
simply leaves me

> *replete*

Past 2 a.m.: you know
what is signified

…struggling in sweat-soaked sheets:
> *Who is drowning?*

But in the subsequent mourning
blood on the walls
rally for gilt frames

…would love to penetrate
 a rainforest
with you, to save you from
the bloodletting of mosquitoes
Fed on milk, my veins
are always sweet

Are you laughing
behind your closed door?
Do your palms lift themselves
(of their own accord)
to lie against
the cool walls of
your monastery?

My heart maintains its own
armor. My blood is blue
> *O my Love—*

Reach for the brass
blocking that keyhole

(ADULTERY

We met at an angle

Waves recede as secondary acts
        (then ~~repeating~~ weakening reproductions)

I did not expect an antique mirror

A thought might be fleeting but still scar

Efficiencies leave invisible wakes

Some mornings offer surcease with the tinkling of high piano notes—they thread their way through my veins—make me arch my back as my cats do when they pause to look with disdain—

—when my reflection is snagged, you see, I am drawn only to how startled I am—around the bend looms something big and bright—in the scent of wet earth, the clinging of dark leaves, the sound of fireflies mating, the thinly slivered moon, there had been no premonition—

(PROFILES

A lone tree rose like an empty flagpole

I detested my attempt to measure intimacy

Boulevards are best at night—dimness
caresses anyone. I could walk forever
until I am eating a mango in Harlem
where I avoid women's eyes
as they always make me cry

I recall Manila—its lost generation
hugging ashed corners of hopeless streets

      where women no longer wear their hair up…

Oh, Eileen, why step on fallen
branches, their sounds cracking air
like the edges of blades against eggs?

Mothers *must* let go …

(COROLLA

Sometimes I pray
Love is always haggled
     before it becomes

Certain thoughts occur only to those
entranced by the layered auras of decay

"I have no use for calm seas
though I appreciate a delicadeza moonlight
as much as any long-haired maiden"

My people are always hungry
with an insistence found only in virgins and fools—
     let the definition of "holiday'
     become the temporary diminishment
     of hostile noise

Let preference become
the position of an ignored chandelier

Riposte? Discover the limitations
of wantonness only through listening—
     there is no value to negative space
     without the intuitive grid

Yes: the girl
in me is a country
of hammocks and waling-waling orchids
In it, I forget the world
's magnificent indifference

Throughout this land—
     this archipelago—
I can silence afternoons
              —oh!—
with a lone, fragile finger

(GREY, SURREPTITIOUSLY

I am not exhausted

I—the one steeped in pacing perimeters—
conjure mists over the East Side. They
swathe the total territory in a wool suit
evoking post-Soviet cities where
tiny pastries waited silently behind glass

Unexpectedly, patchouli and cinnabar
begin lingering in air—I feel the birth
of pearls in ocean beds tended by boys
burnt by a distant sun clamoring for
the intimacy of mortal philosophy

Hit "Pause" in creation—see winter
birch trees stripped of their leaves
            suddenly backdrop to she
smiling as *she* approaches—I wish
to feel my fingers loosening her
jeweled combs, her hair curling
like the breaking of surreptitious surf—
            no words would be spoken
but a window from a suddenly *present*
building would open to loosen faint
piano notes plucked from the highest scale

My fingers willingly freeze against
a stranger's scented cheek—see
her lashes trap a beginning snow—
her eyes, too, would be the deadening
of a river: translucent, *grey*…

(NAMING LUCIDITY

…wind continues—

the universe shakes from its formless assault

A tree loses a limb

Another limb traps a silk, scarlet scarf—it whips
through the air like a student clamoring for attention

In a still-standing house, a stranger
turns on a light: "in that sudden luminosity
leashed tears glint"

Years before a man learned a mirror
can birth a deeply-held flinch
he seated her before cream lace
laden with crystal, silver, ice doves—
he asked her to close her eyes
for a whispered " a moment, Love"—

within a welcomed dimness she felt
the scent of jasmine as an embrace

She felt silk tantalize her naked throat—
        felt Gotan Project's "Una Música
        Brutal" slice open a vein

When she opened her eyes
she saw skeins flattening rubies
to drape over her breasts

She lifted her eyes to his gaze smiling

as if reproductions can deliver on promises

(THE COLOR OF A SCRATCH IN METAL

Imagine the taste of silver, nickel, chrome…

Imagine the taste of a scratch in mercury…

Which would melt black Tahitian pearls—
chemicals or emotion? The question
quivers her fingers into stroking a raven,
its throat, its wings, its most fragile throat…

If a pear was a color, she feels
it would be how shadows glide
across his unshaven chin
If passion was a color, she feels
it would be black sand encasing
a hidden beach behind a cave
wall kissing a sunlit ocean…

"What is seeing?"

It is how he saw her notice
the strain of his effort
not to touch her nearby pulse

but remained sculpture
so that the price he would extract
later amidst twisted bed sheets
would be radically high—

as unforgiving as a sniper's eye…

(EULOGY

…consistently wear city skylines as necklace, bracelets, tiara…

to feel stars as close to me as the speed of light is intimate—
you are an embrace I glean across an archipelago
: there is no edge between us
    not even the shut gate to a Paradise we have only witnessed in a book

We shared vitello tomato in a Roman courtyard
the milky-white sauce camouflaging a peppery bite—

You smiled when my fingers lined through the calm Ganges
as pilgrims raised their eyes to dawn—

When I saw daylight ripple silver across the Lonoan Strait
I longed for you in Boston staring through snowflakes—

"I could feel your heartbeat against the palm
I raised, askance, to block the sun"

Once, a man raised a sword at an enemy made invisible
by the curvature of the vessel—you loved the disappearance
of conflict when your hands turned the pot
to a shift in emphasis focused instead on a dancer
continuing to dance despite the presence of a warrior
: *memory* is a controlling agent—
your finger traced a vein, its protrusion helpless…

"Radiation seduces me by bleaching bones
                            into light!"

You said you met yourself in the dark moss
climbing the pink walls of Alhambra
surrounded by ancient hills whose people
have perfected suffering. I say,

A blind member of the French resistance
insisted on learning dance to obviate
the strange rhythm of strangers' boots
and unfamiliar tobacco colonizing
the stones of Paris—
                   a sunlit sensibility
can pervade reality instead of dreams

Now, *let us be fearless…*

(THE BEGINNING

… a journey but only to the fringe of danger?

Language does *not* want only language

Living as more than a sniper's quick retreat

Language does *not* want only language

A life's tchotchkes to be more than pastel
jailed behind glass, jailed into memory

Language does *not* want only language

See a tapestry and *feel* the prick of the needle

Language does *not* want only language

Remnants create rainbows, angels, non-primary colors, martyrs, orphans,
    serial killers

Language does *not* want only language

Scent an ocean breeze and see an island beyond vision, beneath the fall of the
horizon—scent the presence of a man who will not give up the effort defined as
the opposite of knife handles with no blades, novels missing their ending pages,
earth hollowing under the onslaught of tears—her lover knows that, out of
control, she would be glorious—

Language does *not* want only language

Years would pass before she would realize that she should have been kind
    in a prior life

Language does *not* want only language

Kindness would have transcended much that is visible and more that is not

(THE SOULFUL UNIVERSE

Her skirt flutters
        with random breeze
You sense honeysuckle—

Her eyes kiss
        before she reaches
for a container by her feet—

You are still smelling honey
as she douses herself—

You believe you are in a dream
when she lights a match
            then…

Run towards her
        as if she knows the answer
to that non-theoretical question
            "Can life be decontextualized from inheritance?"
But a glass wall halts your stride—

The most implacable border
can be the invisible
so that nothing is hidden from sight—

As your palms flatten against
lucid, immoveable glass
you feel her say
before pink chiffon disappears
in a blaze so unseemly for its voraciousness,

Let there be grace

—*for Kathleen Chang and Meister Eckhart*

(THE WIRE SCULPTURE

The shadow is thin
but it slices air

The press of approximation
is confident

What is solid is
what is not visible

You look back at
the sculpture

Light has changed
with the progress of an hour

Dwell now on
the simmer in your belly—

how a shadow's imperfection
humbles

recalling now a life
you once wanted

not the existence folding
around your awkward steps

(THE FROZEN GASP

Against the pale blue—
   dowager's paper—
words gestured shards
   from a memory's night

He felt her stirring within
   a shuttered room
hands as restless stalagmites
   scribbling furiously
within the russet beam
   of an ancient lamp
occasionally a pause
   for knuckles to rub
against the blindness of
   lashes clinging together
(helplessly)

I am civilized, he whispers
   at an impassive skyline
I never betrayed a woman
   without first ensuring
her joy in the Aftermath

There was a velvet dress
   whose narrow skirt
sliced itself open
   to reveal marble thighs
There was the glimmer of
   excavated black silk
that would come to approximate
   the surface of her eyes
when he left and she refused
   to cry, to release
defiance…
   These are thoughts articulated
through hindsight

The blue letter lies, flattened
   on burnished leather
stretched over a mahogany desk
   where a sealskin box
offers a stack of business cards
   which fail to identify
him. A gentleman is always more
   than the coincidence
of a name allocated without consent

What good are titles? Especially
        a *President* qualified with Vice?
He identifies all these blows
        pummeling his brain
He flattens fingers against
        a silk tie—despite
the rhythm of geometric patterns
        that would trap
an observer's eye, the tie
        's surface is slippery—
it is facile

(THE EMPTY FLAGPOLES

Why ask for asylum
in places where people seek
to leave?

Where people are pierced
by empty flagpoles?

Where people forget
they deliberately failed
to sign checks before they are mailed?

Where even the tiniest ant
insists on gnawing its bite?

Where black dresses
must be deconstructed
into ruined approaches
of increasingly unfamiliar desire?

… so tired of immolation.
Where

is the next stranger to relish
 my lips
        still painted
        still swollen
        still philosophical
despite my closed eyes?

(APPROXIMATIONS

Exposes
sharp
shoulder
blades—

Gaze
wishes
its
drop

How
replace
solitude
's masks?

Tearing
off
jeweled
combs
not
amoral

Muscles
reveal
ziggurat
when
in
labor

What
significance
to
praising
cathedral
's shell?

Wanting
to
join
women
with
men
constant
ly returning
every
evening—

their
hands
rough
but
trembling
when
approximating
gentleness

Recall
flamenco—
no
matter
how
hard
feet
stomp
to
cleave
earth

The back must be straight

So
many
shadows
blurring
surprised
sections
of
horizons

She
does
not
begrudge
slippery
images
into
plastic-encased
pages

She
does
not
judge
any
blurring

of
memory

(Photos
of)
Wildflowers
cover
the
album—

ever
resplendent
in
sight
despite
their
lack
of
perfume

(JULIET'S SALT

She is persuasive:
salt is sensual

like a girl-toddler
(perhaps naked, except for
blanket dangling from one shoulder)

Feel the scene she's lost in,
directs someone behind the page

It's the same moment of regret
explains the hidden director
as when you utter cruelty
to your father who simply
looks at you, as if to
memorize your relationship
before he leaves the room silently
and in silence

For years, the image of his
face absent of any
expression shall clutch
your heart into an imploded fist

"Oh, Juliet—you lied!"

Salt *is* sensual
but you are still compromised

I'll pick up the beer tab
while you leash your tears
to reach for my hide

With my poker winnings
I'll do more than survive

"Oh, Juliet—those black lies!"

Salt shall sting, then cling
despite your painfully-wide smile

(JANUARY

The roses have emptied
their vase

Yesterday commenced a
new century

Last year's wreaths
have not yet departed—

evergreen, they insist on
scenting light

"as if hope can be a constant,"
whines a memory

She raises her eyes from
a gilded page trapped

in a book bound in cracked leather
to catch

her surprise in a dusty but still lucid
mirror across a stranger's library

Her eyes are wide, seem
helplessly anguished

She turns her eyes
to a new direction:

New York City, on television
the United Nations

plaza where she has felt
solace from

the sight of many nations'
flags waving together in the breeze

"But the flagpoles are empty
in the winter chill, rising
like poorly-lit pencils
attempting to mirror the stoic
skyline across the frozen river"

Bereft, she lies on the silk
rug flattened against

cold marble. Bereft, she shutters
sight

It is in the darkness
that she sees roses

blooming for the first time—
petals exquisite in vermilion

and something more—

Something my future son would label
as he expands his English vocabulary:

ineffable

(FIREBIRD

Perhaps I could silence this firebird swelling my sails with blood, winds, fevers, but even the Seine today was restless
—Anaïs Nin

Broadway clamored—

mist diffused the boulevard's lights

from dimness, hands appeared and disappeared
through movements lacking premonition

Once, a hand revealed pale elegance
with red fingernails without
the tiniest chip on their sheen—

almost, she halted before
the presence of perfection—

almost—

"The destination," she recognized
"arrives at its own time
indifferent to organization
and, often, desire"

The leashed impulse
evoked Rome—

the hours searching for
a rusted iron gate
breaking the reticence
of a high, stone wall—

hours rewarded when
she stepped onto
a rectangle of cracked tiles
where light emanated
only from white tablecloths
reflecting a crimson moon—

scent of cigars—

perfume of crushed cyclamens—

aroma of shaved orange rinds—

The Chianti was harsh
but charismatic

Men left her alone, enabling
her savor of each bite
from a bleeding "rib's eye"

No effort in holding her spine
straight

The present returned
with a man's bowed back—

indifferent to gray
he painted to life
a tango on the sidewalk

she felt the flare
of a woman's lonq skirt
as the artist shifted direction—

she *felt* the jealousy
on the powdered faces
of long-haired women forced to sit
to watch someone else
govern with immodest limbs

The artist had not yet
painted the couple's faces
but she knew their eyes
would be hooded flames

The implication would be clear—

when the tango would evaporate
the woman would lick
her astonishingly crimson lips—

her thickened tongue
would slide
languorously—
                 slide

deliberately

                 fearless

pure animal

(TRAVELER

A simple but hard-fought realization:
the smallest thing can cause rhapsody

Once, she looked over a stranger's shoulder—
the cover of his book winked at her
with a long absent intimacy
through the image of a wall cracked

to enable a sun ray's spotlight on a violet wildflower

A book. Its binding a ruler of sapphire
as vivid as the blue she now seas:
                              the Aegean see

where bronzed men move busily, all
beneath her and the sun

except for one who climbed
a steel ladder to offer
figs split to sprawl on ice

If *Identity* cannot be fixed
does that mean *Self* must fragment?

The air is warm. *Physical*

She recalls a general whose goal
was an impermeable world
But what is compassion?
Must desire always entail
a loss of innocence?

Figs stain fingers purple
Slowly, eyes hooded, she suckles

                         Lingers…

She has received as much
attention as she has given
to a world insistent
the universe is mere inheritance

The horizon intrudes
with a sleepy sun
Blood rushes as the sky
accepts red. Suddenly

a string of lights blaze
overhead to outline the masts

evoking New York City's skyline
compelling her wonderment

at her lips, promiscuous
but never ever having formed
the words to define *Home*

(SECOND PLACE

Before her, untouched
café au lait
presents a surface
imploded into a knothole

She lifts her eyes
for consolation
towards the window
but the glass offers
a reflection of her
gaze: no conclusion

A shadow hovers—
she refuses attention
She knows the dim shape is the fake
cowboy who had leered
from across the room

With the interruption's
departure—even as she
is uncertain about her life
's narrative flow—
the occupant of a birdcage
nearby begins to sing

She decides to try
                            again

But when she turns
smiling towards the song
she sees the bird
crooning towards
mere mirror,
                    receptive
with its avatar tune

Once more, she feels
betrayed by illusion—

This is how she created
a reality of ignoring
café au lait
until it jelled into
the surface of an
interior flaw

Perhaps nothing has
changed its cream
-y feel along the edges
of her tongue. But
she anticipates its warm
slide down her throat
no longer will be
a mother's comfort

even as she would
be forced to swallow

(LIES

… beloved Someone asked
a question involving *Love*

failing to camouflage
his true intent
Months collapsed before
she realized a mere
affirmation would
have been the kindest gesture

She heard the hotel
concierge's advice—
even paused amidst
a silk Persian rug
to turn his words over
in her mind as if
the forms formed
a book with velvet
covers compelling perusal

Then she loosened
yet one more advice
from her thoughts
as debris she could
and did deposit
into an onyx ash
-tray winking under one
of the lobby's chandeliers

"Inhale / Exhale"

The day changed
outfits to feature
her proclaiming
through the shield
of a telephone:
*I just returned
from Tunisia—how
jovial it was!*

She had ended night
with a command to
recall her favorites
among his traits—

the emeralds for his eyes

his anticipation of
her longing for Solitude
the wideness of his
ambition, the scope
of his intellect
and most of all
his lack of fear

If she ever bore
children, she would do
so only for him
(fearless, green-eyed lawyers)—

she was confident one
would become the
youngest President of
the United States

Pause. Sip tea. She
glances at the window

Watching her
                    unrelentingly
her reflection on
lead-framed glass
whispers, loses
prettiness among the cracks

You silly girl. You
are going to end
up alone, alone
alone

(NOBILITY

Suffering never matters when publicized

Diamonds (or handcuffs) never complete a bed

Introductions never suffice

Snowfall evokes Africa—
she once straddled a man there
for access to his blanket's palate
threads defining all of the primary colors
as well as what leaves color speechless

She welcomed the grittiness of fabric
against her knees, ignoring the clench
of his teeth upon her breasts

She was determined to live in Technicolor

In New York City, the snow is never pure—
she loves the effect of contamination
on white

She longs for surprise

long alien to her since a young poet
declared within the fogged world
        of an older century:
I write from a position of happiness—
my way of extending tradition
                                an aesthetic
consideration

She lowers her eyes to his only book—
a single poem long-memorized for
its conclusion: *The physical reality*
of revolution is decadence
The aftermath is what transcends

(ASTHMA

Setting: urban canyon never
been shadowed by an eagle's flared wings

Introduction: she feels what he sees—
the lack of a mountain's jade face
traversed by rivers flowing like my tears
silvered by moonshine *(oh pronoun's
failure to distance!)* whose salt
etched *my* cheeks when I witnessed
an ocean silence him …

                             We share
a fate revolving around water. Whose
liquidity cannot cohere. Into a body
one can touch, entonces, to ignite …

We are all derived from ancient Rome
where drinking wine in lead cups
lowered IQ's: ergo, the lions
dining on ~~Christians~~ humans …

which surfaced in another conversation
about angels plummeting towards jagged
boulders to the operas of lightning and thunder—
falling to own their vision instead of
seeing through ~~God's~~ another's lenses…

"Fear is not a productive Muse …"—

a lesson she mastered by declining
a blindfold before bending …

She undertook that lesson
for manifesting a fable unfolded
on burnt-sienna pages
hidden in a book entitled *PURITY* …

She sees kindness when he ignores
her confession, changing the subject
to a theory that asthma births
itself from an inability to cry
O wheezing sounds by unshed tears
which he recontextualizes into
coal: "Unmined. Unburnt. Heat
~~waiting~~ longing to happen …"

A decade unfolded before she
realized the error of her analysis
He had not ignored her confession—
"Fear is not a productive Muse"—
He had articulated a stone
's potential to glow. To burn
To conflagrate. Like when his lips
never skimmed across a jutting
bone. Water can do more
than evaporate. How now to
survive a poem ending in asthma …

as the narrative aborts, unable to
extend past its Introduction

(BLIND DATE

The vagaries of memory—
you'd considered a prior sighting
inconsequential
                     : *"an insouciant Sancerre"*

Now you feel his touch leap
across a room, the weight
of his fingertips tracing the edges
of your publicly sanguine lips

Dust motes dance in the beams
thrown by a sconce clamped
onto a peacock's florid tail
flowing across silk wallpaper

Why are you stubborn? He asked
just as you said, *I am not stubborn*
Both of you were supposed to sense
the presence of a B-movie camera
then smile after this overlap

We were promised a sunset, he said
when you would have walked away
He nodded towards a waiting
window framed in violet velvet

I didn't lose that badly in poker
you replied but moved towards his
request. Unblinking stare. He should
have spanned your wrist with one hand

He watched you as you watched
a sun die by painting its rubicund
departure across your tender face

Ripeness—against this memory
you take your first sip of a golden wine
nicknamed by commerce as "God's nectar"
Its coldness then warmth
down your throat brings you
forward to the future

where he would take the folds
of a hovering drape and swaddle
it around you as if you were
an infant. *Even violet* can

be gentle, he would whisper
Unexpectedly, you would feel
his fingers tremble
behind velvet camouflage

to spark your heart finally
into breathing. When you
finally would lay your lips
against his, offering a door
he would know can be keyed
open only by his tongue

it would be the appropriate decision
so that civilization aborts
its potential
as an endangered species

(HOW CYBERSPACE LOST MIDNIGHT

In another dimension there existed petals
clinging to a wet pavement
forlorn in their solitude
but insistent with their grasp

She is familiar with departures—
the loosening of embraces
the forfeiture of birth places

In another dimension, a monk
smiled *forever* at her, making
small huts, large bells, whiskered
goats and gnarled trees disappear
until all she could witness was
the monk's body interrupting
a charred horizon. She held on

to the monk's smile until
a swath of his red robe fluttered
to distract her gaze towards
cotton so soft she felt it as
silk. Nor did she need it to skim
across her cheek to receive
the resuscitation of a caress

The "Internet" intervened

Every e-mail cackles: I am
where no man (sic) has gone before

Insomnia no longer exists

In the ensuing blur of meaning
she launched a message through
its black hole that compelled
poets across eight continents to
reply with agitated fingers

But she is still waiting for
the new world of new words
that would compel her to pull
the emergency rope that halts
the train she discovered herself
piloting. *Yea, though there are*

bodies laid across the tracks

(UNSAID

Finally, I will leave all
underwear home. I paint
my face if there exists a 1%
chance I will stumble over
you hugging a street grate
over the dragon's breath
of a subway. When I bend
over to feel the gritty air
I will welcome its stinging
caress in the absence
of your hands reaching
for the ribs caging my heart

I will swallow all *that*

Sometimes you complain about gas
bills, hurling me to my knees
If I could save you from
a faceless utility I'd strip
off all masks
                        I'd give you
the ripest plum, ready to split
apart from a thought. I still
would be folded about your tongue

Once, your hand laid a breath
away on an unsuspecting tabletop
A typhoon's premonition arrived
as my teeth shivered, each familiar
as individuals assaulted by
strangers' one-night stands

I get exhausted
                        sometimes
But your most minute of
coughs still makes me run

I long to be air
                        so you
can stride through me
lean through me, dissect me
simply face me—whatever
you want. I have memorized

your rare approaches—they were
approaches even as your gaze
remained brutally consistently blank

(THE INVESTMENT BANKER

A legal pad
's parallel lines
do not shimmer
like the rippling surface
of a river pregnant
beyond water, rushing
towards sea or sky
both the same
from a distance
so distant the goal
is mere projection

He pauses the pen
before a projected
likelihood of error
rather than the probable
relevance of an answer

    *

Astonished, he gazes
at the stillness
of his manicured fingers

He would have forecasted
his emptied palms
would quake over
the stubbornness of time
unfolding, *passing*

    *

His gaze drops to
the circle of diamonds
distracting from the blue
veins prominent on her wrist

He takes a chance
she would depart
if he said, "Yes"

Thus, would simple
discomfort cause
a 2% rise in
the unemployment rate
of a country whose

name he once struggled
to pronounce
with elegant accuracy

*

The Chairman's wife
smells expensive
Her emerald earrings
tinkle like wind chimes
His breath flutters
like a Trochilidae's
wings while the Chairman
maintains a smug grin
with zero effort

*

English, German, Chi-
nese. Six newspapers
Daily morning reading
after a shave and
a mirror that reminds
his eyes are covered
by thin, red cracks

*

An officemate arrested—
an event failing to console
the parents of a
young, blonde boy
sheeted by leather
and hanging
in some warehouse
adjacent to some tunnel

*

A parent's tears cannot
change his position
of indifference over
certain compulsions

*

At 4 a.m. he is released
to be alone walking
the streets. He believes

the hour offers too many
excuses for loneliness. Now

he is walking after an
unseasonal rain that's
cleansed the light, shined
the pavement and returned
his faith in dignity

He looks forward to winter
when snow will cover
the city. Especially blizzards
with the constancy of
its snow; white never fails
to cling as he walks
within their midst. Sincerely, he
feels for white:
Such a lovely feeling!

      ::

Such a *lovely* feeling:

How Roses Became Ferocious

    The secret to transcending panic
    is theater—

    Ignore memory's stagnant
    gleanings, leavings—

    Always believe in ~~evolution~~ existence—

    Savor your bed
    trashed from his hand
    and lips on your flesh
    for you are awake
    for the first time in decades—

    Finally, a poet discovers
    the heart in an owl
    (thank you, Anne Gorrick!)—

    Those black motes in eyes
    spreading while we sleep
    define absence
    not evaporation but original lack

of vision
which is nature that should not be
questioned—

And when one refuses
in gratitude
to eliminate the dying rose
from the vase
expect other blooms
to hasten their demise
to mere perfume—

Retain the faith:
we all can be better
truly
as we are

(THE SECRET OF HER HAPPINESS

When she first discovered
bliss
it was inappropriate

surfacing right after
felling her mother
to her knees. She was
oblivious for she was 16
as she stood on a stool
overflowing with pink polyester

Her mother bowed her head
to pin the dress care-
fully to shorten its hem
Looking down at her
mother she noticed a
hairless area on the scalp
of one she had considered—
resented for being—invincible

Never had her mother
looked so naked

as if her mother did not possess
two university degrees, a house
with no mortgage, the sagacity
to differentiate between cruelty
and "magnificent indifference"

Yet the daughter stayed her
hand that would have reached
forward to raise *Mama*
from her knees, to empty
her Mama's mouth of pins

Bliss deferred only temporarily
the start of a series
of dreams, always ending
with waking to discover herself
sitting in the middle of
the bed, sheets flung off
her body, fingers still
twitching from the root
of this dream: a physical
memory of caressing her
mother's pink scalp, such

fragile flesh except for
a single strand of hair
lying across the exposed
landscape: a thin strand
of hair mimicking a welt

that simply refused to abate

(MY SAISON BETWEEN BAUDELAIRE AND MORRISON

I would have to find someone who would follow me in my wanderings.
—November 10, 1890 letter from Arthur Rimbaud to his mother

You deconstructed rainbows
to assign colors to vowels

Rock and roll loves you
as do spies. Adolescents
become arsonists chasing
your fire. As for absinthe?
You recognize it as approx
-imation: the pox of a lie

I know what turned you
into a businessman (I have
worn that silk and wool)
Ledgers categorize, then count
Calculations do not feel
nor fold from the ripple
of a breeze or fall before
the sight of tiger *butterflies*

Fold around me (I beg
you). Accompany my midnights
For you I search for
lovers who send me red roses
whose scents I inhale
as I turn their bodies upside
down. I hang them on
flaccid doorknobs. Against
their tarnished metal, petals
flutter, stiffen, die all
for a consequence of living
forever in rapture—that
full bloom, its unrelenting
-ness. Its rapturous bloom
Its red unrelentingness
Its rawness unrelenting…

(THE 11TH WEDDING ANNIVERSARY

A house suffocating from the verb
of emptiness—

within shadows dust curls into fists
piling pyramids onto newly-stark floors

while she stands in the middle
of a foyer, as silent as
the reproach of walls where holes
widen helplessly, nails begin
to rust and no rainbows attempt
suspension (immortality) in lost
beams of light

                that slide off
his posture, spine straight as
an empty flagpole. Surely
there is a tale here, even as it
insists on eliding her tongue—

perhaps how she loves to wander
empty streets at dawn. Once
she saw another quickly turn
left rather than allow their walks
to parallel (*oh she understands!*)

Sometimes one simply must flee
from what one loves the most
(*oh the poet's daughter understands!*)—

the importance of the dissonant
note

(MUSE POEM

Days in a dusty room—the air
lit only with a computer's glow
while stacks of books melt
                              into the shadows

This is the way it should be

Eyes monopolized by a parallel
universe where silence owns no
color. No reason to censor
mountain from saffron, sky from
celadon, boulder from lavender
bougainvillea from cobalt, grass
from ebony, diamond from cerise
you from me. Me from you

Nothing must be silenced. There
must be color, even with
deliberate recollections of fear

with the color of **Wet:** bitter-
sweet, bloodshot, blooming
blush, brick, burgundy, cardinal
carmine, cerise, cherry, chest-
nut, claret, copper, coral, crim
-son, dahlia, flaming, florid
flushed, fuchsia, garnet
geranium, glowing, healthy
inflamed, infrared, magenta
maroon, pink, puce, rose
roseate, rosy, rubicund, ruby
ruddy, russet, rust, salmon
sanguine, scarlet, titian
vermillion, wine …

And the color must be clear
enough to be transparent
A Taoist shaman reminds:
"Bright pure color represents
the virtue." Nothing must be
silenced. There must be color

still satin with the shine
from where all rivers originate

(THE LAMB

She anticipates his departure
thus acts in self-defense

He had hoped to prolong
their "welcomed conflagration"

But she wanted time to
stop
       with him, *his eyes*

The dream is solid, no
longer open to revision—

a book-lined room, feet
atop a damask-covered
ottoman, fingers waltzing
to notes interrupting air

Perhaps a high note would
evoke regret—he plans to
survive. Perhaps a high note
would evoke her—he would
survive *that*, too. And if

an heiress props her innocent
face through the 16th century
mahogany doorway, her face
would be as blurred as his
sight is clear on what exactly

required no fire to be sacrificed

(TAUROMACHIA

Her father loves a story
he claims to be about her—

She is a toddler with
ribbons threaded through her hair
in a white eyelet dress
lace edging her pink socks

She is propped on his knee
as they sit in the shade
offered by a star-apple tree

She gurgles with glee
when they rub noses
rub-a-dub-dub. Her
chubby fists clutch his fingers

as if she will never release her hold
on him despite any mistake
he will make as a father

But she was not born
innocent. *I was not born…*

Place your finger in the midst
of my palm. Feel there
the pulse where my lifeline
ends. There, the pulse is
a gypsy flamenco. My

dress is cut from violet
leather. Underneath, thin
slivers of fuschia silk
and a green tattoo of
a thorn to discover only
when intimacy is ~~unmediated~~ unmitigated

I almost asked you—
for I know you want this
invitation—to join me
as I hunt myself…

Still, let us go stray
only after concluding
implacable business:

How must she hide from her
father that she prefers
her particular difficulty
to the legacy he wishes to
provide? How can she

say *that* when he does not
recognize his true legacy
is the entitlement
of certain decisions
including mistakes?

How does one do what one
must do? What is it that

one must compel?

(MUSTERING

It only takes one person
to bring the world to ruin

The animals, too, would entreat
with wet, intelligent eyes

Where are the white blossoms
on the cherry trees, the kind

-ness in a gaze? Am I
not the fool in King Lear's

court? Whose discernment
is constant, ever feeling

the presence behind tapestried
walls? Look at the eyes

frozen in the mirror. They
wish to fall. But, *Darling,*

how to make them muster
beyond simply the stall…

(AMBER

Blossoming from the sky's embrace
she desired

remaining at this wave-less shore
for offering *suspension*

Ground rose to hide
the flame trees

which dropped rubicund
blossoms on

her cheeks when she tilted
face towards

a bird's cry. She welcomed
their perfume

that would come to scent
the rest of her sunsets—

she treasured any source
of color

for lighting her dreams
She believed

a sunlit sensibility is
an admirable goal

But is the right answer
a longing

for becoming a fossilized
secret within

the immoveable embrace
of gold?

She believes this suspension
lit as if

by an immortal flame
would be

Beauty unable to lose
its luster

despite the unrelenting advent
of Karma

(RESPECT

Counting how
bricks form
the building across Broadway

you failed to appreciate
my addictions. Feel
the apples falling with
-in orchards upstate—
when vinegar begins
tainting the air
it will be discordant
but also please

"And the rain continues so!"
I long for anonymous
traffic to release
the broken roofs
formed by umbrellas
with broken spines—how
long must servitude
be forced?
Search
for consolation by
"looking between raindrops"

This is where fragmented
syntax fails to suffice

I, too, might as well die
by moaning through a fado

Or be an old man huddling
in confidence with a bartender
as we watch a woman
accompany a guitar. Afterwards

she would join us, ample hips
swaying, eyes looking sideways
breasts robust and proudly raised—
we would greet with respect
our eyebrows would not rise

She, on purpose, we would not
suspect

(LATIN

As introduction, a necklace of rubies

But she replied, *I have never favored
men on their knees*

Postscript: *I prefer my stones
at maximum hardness*

But he knew as he departed
diamonds would not have guaranteed

Worse, he felt her gaze
(on his dwindling, suited back)
and it lacked enmity

In his absence, she reached for
a decanter and poured amber
into crystal. She has ~~tamed~~
trained herself to be objective
But she coughed over her
first swallow and recoiled
at surprise, then reared

at the reflection trapped by
the unexpected mirror of a window

before it dissipated at the sun's
shift to angle light anew

As often occurs unbidden
the fresh memory recalled
an older memory stained

by pain: lightning cracking
a summer night in Abiqui—
she had reached for it
and been surprised when
her fingers touched something
tangible that was supposed
to be simple light

Beneath a new source
for fragmented vision
she began to consider
whether she should attempt
something else. If, say,

the chandelier fell, it
could murder. She began
to consider:

                        a path that
yet again, led astray into:

What about sweetness?

(THE FAIRY CHILD'S PRAYER

Because the sky
can never margin
my desire, I

raise my hand
to you, thereby
compelling the
swoop of jade eyes
cobalt breast, ebony
feathers, cruel eyes

I have emptied
my bag of tricks
released barbed wire
from tattooing
my left wrist

choose to believe
all Life ravishing
even its shadows

The Milky Way
that grazes the Maori
mountains of your
birth equals the
silvery cascade
threading through my hair
as my mind's eye
wanders through a
universe I once thought
I inherited instead of
Something I can paint

You nudge my memory
for afternoons of
pollination: lemon dust
attaching to opened
flowers whose petals
form light's prisms

The sky, you teach
shall never need
to drop for me to
feel its blanketing

embrace. My tongue
shall become another
bolt of white velvet
I shall swathe
around our planet
and hold as an infant
against my milk-laden
breasts. When the
horizon stuns again

it shall be from your
sumi ink evoking
my hands when, for
the first time, they shall
be graceful as they
dance anew the ancient
form: "Fairy Child
Praying to the Goddess
of Mercy Kuanyin
Shao Ling Kung Fu Fist"

(MY STATEN ISLAND FERRY POEM

To be taken up higher and higher by uneven stone stairs and to stand there with your heart beating outside the gate of the near world. To gather laurel and marble for the white architecture of your destiny. And to be as you were born, the center of the world.
—Odysseus Elytis

In Tuscany, fires
amid castle stones
pockmark hillsides

To see these fires
is to see the stars
of dying men
in white, tight shirts
toiling past midnight
in Manhattan skyscrapers

Are you looking
at me as I tilt
my face elsewhere
to hide the yearning
in my gaze?

A cloud lifts
to unclothe the moon—
its silver shadow
ripples across water
loosening languid drops
of mercury—
                              gasp
with delight as heat
burns white into our sight

With its minute swells
the river is lyrical

All I hear as fires
burn in Tuscany
is the rush of memories
awaiting birth

All docks approach
                              eventually

I peer through the dark
and latch onto
another breeze

soaring to bring
the perfume of magnolias

Straight ahead is
a sunlit day
with a sky whose
press against the horizon
is as careful as you

Thus, the horizon remains
invisible, masking
where journeys end
despite the firm hope
dampening my eyes
determinedly open

(THE DESTINY OF RAIN

A single brushstroke
united the separate
panels of rice paper
as fragile as existence

A brushstroke rose
until it thinned
into smoke

His friends were calm
at discerning smoke
its ending invisible
against the white

while scenting sampaguita
for its petals, too, are so white
they manifest the metaphor
for *Innocence*

The mirrors in his eyes
have pained all
of his friends—the fragile
ones felt blood escape
from their faces
though they knew
he was only attempting
to embody smoke

Inevitably, he will whiten
into the clouds
and the unanswered question
will be, "Might Justice
be colored white?"

Still, in an obvious lapse,
he once gasped out
the word, "Love"—
a compulsion that, for
his friends, paid for
an eternity of forgiveness

So it came to pass:
his friends happily reconciled
to the destiny of rain

As for her? (The Love of His
Life?) Storms have always
been in unapologetic season

(THE CONTROLLING AGENT

"The past is thick"

He was supposed to
carve *Innocence*—
a boy with plump cheeks
squatting breathlessly
by a river lacking ripples
so as not to disturb
a bird perched on his shoulder

But the artist affirmed
his avocation by
also carving a lifted wing
as if the bird is about
to fly for the illusion
known forever as "sky"

The observer controls
the subject unless
another observer understands
history. *For the present
is thin, and the past thick…*

(THE RECEPTIONIST

Cosmopolitan, she ruminates

on "the cleavage of toes"—

November is aghast, as
ever, with the latest bellow
-ing wind. She cannot
recall when she last
witnessed a lurid sky—

she has chosen against
the best of psychology—

she chooses friends only
among those alarmed
by a lack of elevators—

still, in her beloved penthouse
where she feels each sky
-line as a zirconium necklace

she looks at a dead
light bulb she cannot reach
to replace, where the walls
won't stop giggling forth
their cruel question: *Where
are the giants who once
walked the earth?*

                    *

When the walls shall begin
to sob forth their question
she shall paint her toenails
scarlet for *Eros* has yet
to betray her, cosmopolitan
despite the job she chose
for its absolute lack of challenge

*Bring it on, ye histrionic
-ally bawling walls!*

*I receive, I am
the receptionist. I am
receptive. I receive…*

(IMMEDIATELY BEFORE

Winter, as ever, proceeds
at its own pace—

Nor does intention
ever suffice—

She, as ever, chooses decisions
as keys bejeweled by hedge funds
to open closets freezing with Russian sable coats—

His hair mirrors the color
of the fur she never wears—

the complexion of heated butter
just before a total meltdown—

That immediately before

(THE CASE FOR APLOMB

Truth insists—

Dusk defined as
grey-haired women un-
binding combs seeded
discretely with pearls

Somewhere in SoHo
a nude clenches eyes
to paint a floor magenta
with glistening hair
as witnessed by men
in Wall Street suits
Swiss deep-water watches
and Greenwich wives

I would like to fall
in love with policemen
who need not be American—
no continent can contain
my fidelity delineated
only by boozy notes
finishing the moans
of sweaty, heavy women—

these earnest women flit
between sequined dresses
and church choir gowns
Their capacities heighten
my hunger and I long

to unite the pristine convex
with the glorious mess of concave

(FRANZ KLINE KINDLY SAYS ABOUT THREE GESTURE-LADEN BRUSHSTROKES

Can a politician avoid
mastering barter
when he (always a *he*)
inherits a country
pulsating with industrial
waste? And the view
across a border is
the abundance of Brass
-ica napus, Thiaspi alp
-estre and Festuca rubra?

Allow the heart its complete
measure of each decision
Allow the mind the implication
of the Kundiman, a love
song rooted in a military ballad
>   *As she fell, she looked*
>   *behind her at the frozen*
>   *silhouette of a man*
>   *who chose not to follow—*
who taught lucidity by noting
"Blow up the world if
you must. But avoid ambiguity"

How foolish to deny
a snake the swallow
of its tail. A circle
reveals perfection and
days should somehow begin
and reveal
>   *something not elsewhere*

(ABANDONING MISERY

"dissonance may abandon miserere"
—Barbara Guest

To consider butterflies
predictable
is to comprehend Beauty—
the flit of wings carving
a random path
but with its conclusion
inevitable: attain then sip
from a country's sweetest bud

"All ages are impressionable"—
one could be sipping from
the shimmering air
over a datsan in Siberia
—three taps, a wheel turns—
yet the West could surface
from an impassive stone Buddha

She sings lullabyes
to resurrect beloved parents
bring them to ballrooms
ablaze from chandelier lights
gleaming crystal, reflections
from gold-edged mirrors, sheen
of a band's brass instruments
and, finally, the love in her eyes
When men loosen their chains
to dive off ships for her
songs, when she bares her
heart to rock's jagged spears
her smile comprehends Beauty—

Absolutely no need to apologize …

(INSOMNIA'S LULLABYE

I tear strips from the sky
to peel off the stars
a lesson from jeweled
pieces of candy
on wax paper

I have wondered
what the sky hides

Tear the sky to discover
the sky bleeds

(as you once bled when I
tore your hands away
from my waist
as you attempted
to console)

Note the frigorific
blast of wind
across the midnight
-purple surface of the lake

Tear off another strip
to discover sleep, gift
of unexpected memory
of Michelle, Barbara, Joey
feeding me *balut, sinigang*
white rice and *longanisa*—

All this was foretold
by a haruspex
but as he remains quivering
behind the immense night sky

I had to experience
—the ineffable!—
to cure
insomnia

                    to remember how
moonlight on Fifth Street
(Berkeley, California)
silvered everything it touched—

like the sticks of Kali

and those making them dance
with, not against, the wind—

like the windchime
and the four poets
it delighted with its song

*—for Michelle Bautista, Barbara Jane Reyes and Joey Ayala in a dream-period long
ago…*

(RAPUNZEL, ENRAPT

"stairs rising to platforms lower than themselves
Doors leading outside that bring you back inside
—Clifford Geertz, on Michel Foucault

A thousand diaries
unread after they were written—
I offer this poem instead
to mark their existence

A poem that speculates
she released her hands
from their velvet gloves

that she smiled
as she shivered

that she lifted skirts
to flee from guides
dispatched by a godfather
(an emperor ruling
a troop of retired generals)

that a man once buried
his face into her shaking hands

which would later clamber
down a rope
treasuring the roughness
against her soft palms

that she chose a path
opposite in direction
from the man's choice
when he departed

that, once, he looked up
as he left
          (determinedly? helplessly?)
and she displayed
no bitterness

that books had taught her
how Egyptians memorized
intangible light, thus
revealing earth's profile
to be a curve

that after she stopped
writing in diaries
she learned the pleasure
of the gasp

that as she continued
to gasp she began
to run. That she ran

and ran until she began
to *feel* his ship
disrupting the horizon

that a sheen broke
across her brow
as she felt her lips
begin to part

that she gasped
and ran

until, enrapt, she
realized her future
will begin with her
decision to release her
hands from their blindfold

that she heightened rapture
with a deepening knowledge
that she is getting there

       that she is going there!

that she heightened rapture

into the mating
of a white dove and red rose

but the red remained dominant
undiluted by *Innocence*

(AGAINST DISAPPEARANCE

"A stake, an axis is thus driven into the earth in order to mark out the boundaries of the sacred space in many patriarchal traditions. It defines a meeting place for men that is based upon an immolation. Women will in the end be allowed to enter that space, provided that they do so as nonparticipants."
—Luce Irigaray

Post-tower, Rapunzel
admires the welts
beloved stigmata on her palms

She allows tears
to water red tracks
for pain to heighten
the occasion of freedom

It will never cease
to stun—the effect
of a blindfold falling
even if the mask
had been silk and lace
festooned with diamonds
rubies emeralds pearls

The shadow of a dove
(in a flight she would
later describe as "ecstatic")
interrupts her reverie, makes
her tears evaporate. She
wipes her palms against
the velvet covering
her thighs. She lifts her
skirts to dance down a path
whose unknown destiny
she welcomes for its dance

She dances with a skein
of silver butterflies appearing
from nowhere to coax out
her laughs. She dances
until an old dwarf
from another fairy tale
pops up his head by the bend
of the road to glare, "Who
are You?" She proclaims
with glee, with pride: "Rapunzel!"

To which the dwarf snorts
"Nonsense! Rapunzel has long hair!"

She laughs and announces
as she twirls so robustly
her skirts flare high to reveal
legs bare of silk hose
"I cut my hair! Braided a rope
as escape from my turret!"

Amazed, the dwarf said, "How
did you think to strategize?"

Rapunzel stopped her dance
fixed a cold stare at the dwarf
and hissed like Clytemnestra:

When women control their destinies
they exercise a law of nature!
How dare you be surprised!

(RETURNING THE BORROWED TONGUE

warm stones gather the rainfall
speaking a gray language
I've tried to imitate
I read books compiled
From anonymous scrolls
I eat their dust
Hoping to trace
The steps to heaven
—from ": Looking for Buddha" by Jaime Jacinto

Trade one ocean for another
but the waves
     and salt
retain the same pungency

What does it mean, a mirror
asks, to be one's own bridge?

She had to infiltrate a caravan
of students traversing Siberia
towards Lake Baikal
to discover a false memory
of witnessing Lucifer's fall

She realized with sorrow
I can be myself only
in exile. Entonces
comprehension over his refusal
to look back as he depart
-ed for a different ocean
whose salt is familiar
but which he wants to taste anew
whose embrace is familiar
but which he wants to feel anew
whose sun is familiar
but which he wants to kiss anew
by simply lifting his face

He never doubted she would
wait on the other side
of a planet he must circle
until he is felled to his knees

When, on his knees, he still
will continue moving forward
she will be the altar
perfumed by white candles

       —and the blood of fallen
       priests, virgins, poets
       healer-crones, sons
       daughters, bastards
       politicians, rebels, mothers—
that will halt his journey
make him stand, then stay

For this fable, no words

There only is the breaking
of silence, the evenings
of solitary grace in a dim
room, at a desk before
a blank piece of paper
spotlit by a lone lamp
and, yes, one more attempt
with the wake of another
yet the same implacable day

A Note From the Studio

These poems were all "sculpted" out of the prose poems in my first U.S.-published book, *Reproductions of the Empty Flagpole* (1998), many of which were also featured in *THE THORN ROSARY: Selected Prose Poems & New 1998-2010.* While interested readers can look up the prose poems to compare with the verses in *SUN STIGMATA,* for convenience I share a prose poem below that you can compare immediately with its poem-sculpture. I chose the prose poem for "(Approximations" since its poem-sculpture on Page 41—comprised mostly of one-word lines—is as opposite as can be from the prose poem form:

APPROXIMATIONS

She deliberately wears a dress that exposes the sharpened blades of her shoulders and the gold wires piercing her navel. She knows their stares linger, that they wish to dip their gazes lower. No one ever credits her with replacing the mask of solitude with something else. She is judged by the amorality of tearing off the jeweled combs that caged her hair. They believe her to be her red velvet dress, cut, too, to reveal a black butterfly in flight when she ripples a muscle along her thigh.

He refuses to understand why she would leave amidst their state of bliss. When she replies by praising the shell of a cathedral in Barcelona that men failed to complete despite the passing of an entire century, she knows her explanation cannot be clearer. She can feel the workmen's roughened hands, gritty with dust, as they cracked yet another slab of marble. She wishes to be all of the women awaiting their return each evening. They would cross thresholds desperate for tubs of steaming water. Afterwards, they would turn first to her before bread, cheese and wine. As shadows darkened, she would feel their rough hands tremble in their approximations of gentleness.

She once found cruelty by cashing in a rare ticket to the fashion shows of Paris. She spent subsequent decades seeking to return. But the earth continued to spin and she has never mastered how to rupture a circle's smooth bend. Then a woman passed through a small town in the Midwest where she stayed for a summer. (She can never remember the name of this town she felt compelled to taste because it has never been desired: its people always left.) The woman recalled how difficult it was to overcome years of ballet training. I would rather dance the flamenco: always, the back must be straight no matter how hard the feet stomps to cleave the earth. The woman obviated Paris. Still, she did not expect her heart to be sundered by the sight of the woman's hair in the wake of her departure. It was tossed carelessly by a harsh wind.

Now, she is distracted by a new man because she knows it is merely a matter of time before he flees. She considers her goal to be modest: that breezes contain themselves during the day he departs. When he leaves, she wishes that day to be sunlit and the horizon a clean line. She hopes to memorize the shadow of his departure cutting neatly across the horizon. She does not want a random wind to blur the edges of that memory she will slip into a plastic-encased page in a sterilized photo album. Resignedly, the album always waits. It is covered by pictures of flowers in full bloom, resplendent in sight despite their lack of perfume.

Finally, of interest perhaps to other poets or to students, maybe my prose poems (or yours!) can source some of your own sculpted poems. If so, feel free to share your efforts with me at GalateaTEN@aol.com.

Eileen R. Tabios

ABOUT THE SOURCE MATERIAL
Reproductions of the Empty Flagpole

Reproductions of the Empty Flagpole is full of lovely, surprising conjunctions: "the sound of fireflies mating, the thin sliver of a distant moon, … no premonition for such blinding light."
—Arthur Sze

Her poems allow our minds to be excited twice, by the psychological and artistic reference points from which the words zoom-out like handpicked bees from a hive, and by the vivid hum of the poems themselves demonstrating a captivating, utterly original imagination. In her lines, which are at once strict and sensual, Eileen Tabios inserts stingers barbed with wit and political incisiveness. The crisp, almost scientific clarity of her syntax is relentlessly undermined by fabulous leaps from sentence to sentence, by paradox, radical juxtaposition, lurking sexual innuendo, and unpredictable narrative swerve. Her is as poetics of social and cultural interrogation, in which she succeeds in uniting what she would call "the convex with the concave." *Reproductions of the Empty Flagpole* will stand you straight up.
—Forrest Gander

"And what is seeing?" asks Eileen Tabios in this volume of prose meditations on travel, eros, art, and innumerable other subjects, objects. Tabios' answers—her seeings—come out of an amazing range of references, from Buddha to Salman Rushdie to Anais Nin to Anne Truitt to a nameless investment banker; from the Ancients to the Romantics to the Moderns and back again; from the Philippines, as from the United States. Through it all, reader and writer find themselves "losing uncertainty" through Tabios' "eroticized history," which earns its final exclamation, "worthy is the price: Yes!"
—Susan Schultz

How often do you come across language so lavishly expansive that any description you can think of seems laughably one-sided? Better just to slap a warning label on it: "Danger: Contents combustible on contact with reading. Includes poems so fired up they'll sear your fingerprints off as you feel your way through them (instant identity loss). Others brilliant enough to burn after images into your retina. Handle recklessly if at all."
—Barry Schwabsky

…exposes Tabios's search through history and art to understand her central demands-to perceive freely, to investigate color, to be a fully responsive being. "Can you pay the price for risking perception and imperceptibility?" she asks in "The Continuance of the Gaze," and then answers, "I trust in radiance. Let: Us."
—*Publisher's Weekly*

This is not the world of fixed identities… It's a different world, whose poets are forging a cultural identity that is post-colonial, revolutionary, universal, and peaceful. Theirs won't be a unifying flag under one god, but one that's as various as the hands that raise it.
—Leza Lowitz, KQED Radio Show Pacific Time

Tabios has a remarkable ability to move from the abstract and the intellectual to the sensual and the tangible. She's a poet of the streets, and she's above the streets, in her own head, exploring and mapping her own consciousness where ever it takes her, even into the realm of "psychological insecurity."
—Jonah Raskin, *THE PRESS DEMOCRAT*

…in Tabios' own inexhaustible experiments in the written word all schools and philosophies and deconstructivist axioms can go hang… // Some detractors may label Tabios' work pretentious but that may be just another way of saying it is way ahead of its time and so

would make many a new critic uncomfortable. // Or that she has a big ego which is true of many a controversial and ground-breaking artist. But only in the sense that Mallarme and Valery and the rest of those weird, turn of the last century French poets were ground-breaking and whose very poetry was a way of life.
—**Juaniyo Arcellana,** *The Philippine Star*

Eileen R. Tabios has written a book that will leave you flipping back to the first page in hopes that you have forgotten to read a page, that one or hopefully two of the pages were stuck together somehow, and you have the chance to read more. Ms. Tabios won a National Book award for several poems in this book and one has but to read it to see why. What beautiful and tragic imagery she provides. The language seethes with beauty
—**Chris Mansel,** *The Muse Apprentice Guild*

Unlike most poetry books that are light as feathers, their words and images floating off the page, this one is substantial in every way imaginable. Thick with imagery, subject matter, geography and precise and inspired syntax, Eileen Tabios' work reminds me of going for a swim in the ocean—a complete envelopment in the currents of poetry. There is beauty… but her prose forms also tackle the grim and boding….Tabios' prolific meditations on writing, living and loving in modern times solidifies her role as one of the foremost Filipino American poets of the 21st century.
—**Neela Banerjee, LitPicks: New Books For You To Read,** *ASIAN WEEK*

To my mind, the measure of a poetry book's success would linger over questions of intellectual usefulness—the book's continuing, viable rhetorical challenges. In that sense alone, then, volumes could be written about how and why *Reproductions of the Empty Flagpole* is important both for purposes of study in creative rhetorics or poetics, and as a most satisfying, pleasurable read.
—**Chris Murray,** *Sentence: A Journal of Prose Poetics*

In an age of electronic and "disposable art," where surfing the 'Net is akin to flipping endlessly through cable TV channels in search of reconnection in an atmosphere of isolation (calling to mind Robert Pirsig's line from *Zen and the Art of Motorcycle Maintenance* that looking at nature through the car window is just more TV…), the meditative works in *Reproductions of the Empty Flagpole* defy the reader to simply skim and move on. The hooks are finely barbed and grab you in the deepest places.
—**Joey Madia,** *New Mystics Review*

Eileen Tabios has clearly created something new with this collection of prose poems, and her work does indeed borrow from a dizzying number of other forms of discourse, forms shaped lovingly into gardens that tempt the reader into exploring their verdant depths. But these gardens aren't as benign as they appear at first glance, and we would do well, while walking the paths in Tabios' book, to keep our ears alert for wild, hungry sounds in the shadows.
—**Clayton A. Couch,** *Sidereality*

I can think of Ted Hughes writing these poems, were he to use a female persona with the sensibilities and multi-cultural experience of an Eileen Tabios. Saludos!
—**Luis Cabalquinto,** *OurOwnVoice*

Her poetry exudes unabashed sensuality, artistry, intelligence, and lends itself to a reader's surprise at their own insight…. Tabios is indeed an activist whose medium is her poetry. For the Little Brown Brother to re-write his colonizer's language into unexpected structure and exacting, stimulating prose that comes out as poetry excellence—it is an act of activism in itself.
—**Perla Daley, October 2002 "Book of the Month,"** *BagongPinay*

II.
ABOUT THE COVER

EMMY CATEDRAL'S INVITATION TO HER "DANCES IN THE DARK"

Space is, among other things, a form of abstraction, and, like abstraction, cannot exist on its own in the eyes—or minds—of the beholder. Because once the beholder is involved, a taint (of subjectivity) surfaces and purity is lost.

This doesn't prevent many artists from attempting to know, or create works that manifest, purity, perhaps because many of us strive for the ideal, for perfection, as if it is possible to know these beyond concepts.

What Emmy Catedral does with her search, however, is different from what many artists attempt when such artists believe the artist—via creation—is God. Catedral, on the other hand, searches by giving up the artist-as-God perspective.

This may be paradoxical, given how Catedral once described her intention (in a letter to me) for her series "variations of resistance":

> I have been thinking of a way to introduce my work to you, and I realize that the legal pad series, which I've titled "variations of resistance," is probably the best project to start with. Its inception, or at least the moment I began thinking about the lined page as more than a writing surface was during a panel that you were moderating! It was at AAWW's *Intimacy & Geography* conference, held at CUNY Grad Center, which must have been sometime in 2002. Asked about her writing process, and before she even got into talking about the pieces of paper that she lays out on her table, [poet] Mei-Mei Berssenbrugge replied by calling the page a "plane of consciousness"—thus preferring it to the computer screen. I found it true for myself, that lined or otherwise, the piece of paper allows me small discoveries that would be difficult to come forth on the screen. I can cross things out on paper, connect a word to another, erase, create evidences of thought and response—in effect: palimpsests. With lined paper, however, I can demonstrate even more this control: I can defy the lines, obliterate them as I traverse the plane.
>
> […] And so it came to be that I began to manually alter pages of legal pads: moving the magins, writing against the lines, even cutting out the lines, or filling the page with margin lines.

In other words Catedral admits to beginning her project in part by exercising "control."

But Catedral also came to embrace the subsequent loss of control required by and in her process—a demand that, had she not accommodated, would have prevented her from making her works so effective. It is through that maturation that her manipulated objects grew into Art.

*****

Art can be political but politics is not art. Catedral is a, as the saying goes, "political artist" (though I consider the phrase tautological since I believe all art is political). The political origin can be gleaned from the title of her series itself: "variations of resistance," as well as in how the title doesn't have capitalized letters. Not to title the first letter of words (as often occurs in titles) is to avoid privileging one letter over another. Her political bent is also evident from how she chose to work with legal pads for her series:

> I began thinking about the lined paper as readymade landscapes—that on these leaves of 99 cent store, utilitarian legal pads, I can question designated space lines in the more immediate sense of geography: political subdivisions of land, borderlands, territories, separation walls, and after reading Arundhati Roy, even the big dams. These factory produced yellow planes are not unlike the borders in the world: visible or invisible, they are unnatural, man-made.

Part of what makes Art so thrilling is how its manifestations can transcend the artist's own intentions. Though Catedral (initially) focused on geography and how humans manipulate landscape, I believe her project poses many more implications. Catedral is also resisting notions of silencing, marginalizing, making invisible, dominating, canonizing, colonizing—which is all to say, of Other-ing.

She is concerned with the lofty—Berssenbrugge's avowed "plane of consciousness." But Catedral's material is still the ubiquitous yellow legal pad. This mundane object rarely elicits our attention, serving mainly as a receptacle for our thoughts rather than as an entity with its own integrity(ies).

And while Catedral was just beginning her considerations of the implications of the margin, she thought to look off of the page. Where? She looked down at yet another space to which we rarely offer attention and, indeed, walk on: the floor.

What the yellow pad and floor share in common is partly how they easily symbolize whatever elements a society or culture may least value: whether it's the labor of undocumented immigrants, the opinions of the disenfranchised, or the rights of the impoverished. By drawing our attention to such lowly objects, Catedral ultimately suggests that we to pay attention, and be more caring, as regards our environment.

To make her case, Catedral, however, had to lose control of intention, as I suggested earlier. It wasn't, I suspect, a big leap. For, even in the beginning of this project when Catedral consciously thought of herself as in "control," she already was reconsidering; one of the lines she was scribbling around her manipulated margins were these words by Edward Said (from his book with Jean Mohr, *After The Last Sky*):

> Every direct route to the interior and consequently the interior itself is either blocked or preempted. The most you can hope for is to find margins, normally neglected surfaces and relatively isolated irregularly placed spots on which to put yourself. You can only do so through much perseverance and repetition. So many have already done this ahead of you and in the knowledge that their distinction may well appear at the end and after much effort as a small nick, a barely perceptible variation, a small jolt irony, an imposition, odd decorum.

In other words, she realized that her goal was not the mark she would make, if only because any such gestures by her may be just "a small nick, a barely perceptible variation, a small jolt…" What Catedral understood is the critical role of the viewer to her work. That is, her art cannot be effective as abstract or pure or ideal. They need to be tainted by the viewer's presence, the viewer's perspective. If the viewer is absent, there is no work. The viewer inherently must be present, which is also to say, the viewer is not separate—or Other—from the work itself.

This is the implication of the hope Catedral expressed while still in the early phases of her project: "The work requires close inspection, and I liked the idea of the viewer having to enter the margin in order to see the work. I am developing this into a series of installations wherein the viewers themselves have to physically defy or resist designated space in order to get to my discrete object at the far end of a room (I am thinking short cinder block walls for the next one, or putting blackboards with erasure marks in people's way)."

*****

In May 2005, Catedral was able to exhibit a part of her project in "Geography of Now," a group exhibition presented by The Emerging Artist Coalition and exhibited at Pancake Gallery (New York City).

In planning her part of this group exhibition, Catedral manifested "margins" by first asking the other artist-participants which parts of the gallery they wished to use for their works. Catedral then placed her art in between the spaces preferred by the other artists. She would come to relate this approach to Vito Acconci's thoughts in a prose piece entitled "Life on the Edge: Marginality as the Center of Public Art" (from Tom Finkelpearl's book *Dialogues in Public Art*, as I was just beginning to reexamine the legal pad. From Public Space in a Private Time (http://www.kunstmuseum.ch/andereorte/texte/vacconci/vapubl_e.htm) he writes) including the following:

> Inside the gallery/museum, the artist functions as the center of a particular system; once outside that system, the artist is lost between worlds; the artist's position, in our culture, is marginal. The public artist can turn that marginality to his/her advantage. The public artist is forced, physically, off to the side; the public artist is asked to deal not with the building but with the sidewalk, not with the road but with the benches at the side of the road, not with the city but with the bridges from city to city. Outside and in between centers, the public artist is under cover; public art functions, literally, as a marginal note: it can comment on, and contradict, the main body of the text of a culture.

Thus, Catedral made strips of paper cut along the margins of legal pads and placed them hanging from the gallery's ceiling. The paper pieces hover over the action, unseen unless people look up. Catedral's strategy is smart as the act of looking up can be correlated to paying homage or respect. In other words, the margin-ed paper strips were not just allowed to litter the floor on corners of the gallery room, a position that's more obvious as an aesthetic decision and a locale where dust and dirt also tend to congregate. What is marginalized, in other words, may still deserve honor.

Catedral also placed some of her works in the bathroom, a space not just away from a gallery where the primary activities unfold but a space that is usually hidden from view, and yet where the most basic acts of intimacy unfold, i.e. the release of bodily waste. By locating "art" in the bathroom, Catedral shifts our mental processes from moving into the forefront a space that is typically low in privilege. And why not? What we release from our body also defines who we are, doesn't it?

With her bathroom installation, Catedral draws attention to an area that may not elicit much of our thoughts because, presumably, bathroom-related activities are just diversions from another, and more important, unfolding of our lives elsewhere (beyond the bathroom). In facilitating the expansion of our lucidity to acknowledge that our bodily wastes are part of who we are and how we spend our days, Catedral breaks down borders, or moves and erases what would be sources of marginalization (the bathroom as less privileged than the primary gallery space). Moreover, her process of doubling back to reconsider, essentially, Identity is also aptly manifested by the placement of the work to be reflected in the mirror.

Beyond the bathroom, Catedral involved the exhibition attendees into her works by bringing pads made from the thin strips of paper created from having been cut along the legal pads' margin lines. She asked attendees to write into these thin pads. She then pasted the paper pieces against a pillar or gave the attendees pieces of tape and asked them to tape them wherever they please. Again, the gallery attendees' roles are integrated into the works—indeed, if they didn't participate, no works would come to exist.

How synchronistic that her favorite—and I love it, too—is how someone curled a margin-ed strip of paper (thus hiding what message would be written within it) and that the message is "dancing in the dark" (contributed, as I would later discover, by another Filipina artist and poet Erna Hernandez).

Relatedly, Catedral also noted to me that as she was writing about her project, "I came to a realization that my use of the margin as a subject is possibly even influenced by your bringing attention to the 'footnote.'"

Catedral was referring to a series of "footnote poems" that I conceived to be part of my book *I Take Thee, English, For My Beloved* (Marsh Hawk Press, 2005). In this book, the poems are not laid on the pages as primary subjects. The pages are blank, except for 1-3 lines of a prose poem printed at the bottom of the pages. They are presented as footnotes, but they are the only text available to be read. And just as Catedral asked gallery attendees to write on her margin-ed pads and become part of the art works, the reader(s) of my poems are asked to imagine the stories being footnoted by my poems—theoretically, the readers can be the ones to inscribe on the blank sections of the page, thus showing how I, as the poet, gave up authorial control.

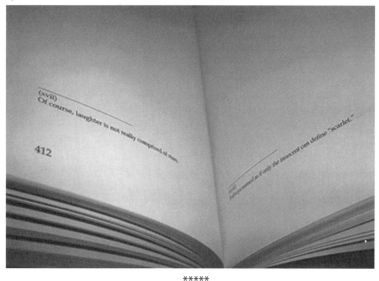

*****

The most effective dancers are often those who give up control of their bodies to the music. It's worth noting the openness with which Catedral engaged in the lessons generated by the actual process of making art. Her openness allowed her to continue extending the path of her series. For instance, at the end of snipping out the margins from the pages of the legal pads, whether the margin as drawn vertically on the left-hand side of the page or by the blue lines drawn vertically across the pages, she was left with much margin-less sheaves of paper.

She didn't dispose of these paper portions which had been incidental to the creation of margin-ed pads. By not trashing them, she also ends up using her meditations on margins to question the categories of what are "considered "trash." Often, what are marginalized are considered disposable elements and Catedral makes us pause again to reconsider our attitudes towards waste—not just items we may put in an actual trash container but also other elements that we consider disposable. Such enhances the political component of her work as disposability certainly relates to values, ranging over whether one, say, should always tell the truth to whether a "living wage" is a viable consideration in determining how people should be paid for their jobs.

Catedral took the margin-less sheaves of paper and created a "Gondwandland" that hearkens, she said, "single continent before man-made borders, political subdivisions of land." She added that she "very consciously did not want to create a perfect yellow ball, as I know a pangea is irretrievable. There are some bits of blue from the lines. The cut-out ones actually start to look green arranged a nest-like pile because of the blue lines against the yellow...this is ongoing. I intend to keep adding to the ball maybe until I go insane, then I will stop. Maybe."

Catedral's vocabulary in desiring and designing Gondwandland is telling: "a single continent before man-made borders [or] political subdivisions of land." Legal pads, of course, are among the most basic tools of the legal profession—including what lawyers and politicians use to define borders.

As she kept layering paper sheaves over the ball to make Gondwandland, Catedral observed that the object "actually start[ed] to look green" and "arranged as a nest-like pile." The result, therefore, is a homage, even if romanticized, to nature before man began imposing its presence. Or, a nest before, inevitably, the nest's residents mature and begin changing the nature of its nests.

*****

Still, one of the most brilliant works from Catedral's series goes back to the roots of her exploration. That is, after cutting out the margins and lines from legal pads, she glued the paper pieces back together. But to do so means that, de facto, margins and lines are created through the seams of the paper sheaves.

The result, while similar to, is different from the predetermined margins and lines on the pages before Catedral began manipulating the pages. This time, the new lines are a function of where the spaces themselves end and overlap, rather than as vertical and marginal lines imposed against the pages and which the users of legal pads are forced to accept with no input as regards their placements.

Consequently, what Catedral illustrates is the integrity of the objects (the pages before a factory arbitrarily lined them) so that Catedral shows how enhanced lucidity facilitates how we may engage with the world more respectfully.

Ultimately, Catedral has taken generally unloved objects (legal pads and the floor) and showed how they can symbolize Love—specifically Love as an infinite expanse. When Love comes with constraints, such borders do not surface as a result of Love's inherent nature but due to any limitations we choose to or inadvertently impose. Catedral then shows how widening our vision inherently expands our capacities to Love.

113

III.
HUMMING A CRITIQUE

HEART POETRY: A CRITIQUE

"you can't leave the theater humming the critique"
—Charles Bernstein

It moves towards
but stutters
like love over a lifetime—

Observation and meditation
if conducted deeply
harvest pain—

Fake flowers
are often too bright
inappropriately so
for grief
(but how else to see
them so swiftly passed
as they blur the edges
of roads continuing on)—

A restless mind
expands vision
unafraid of mess—

Their words—texture—
are ravishing
and ravished—

The poems are quiet
And disquiet—

To see the thing
as the thing itself—

An orphan's rant
for attachment
speaks to desire
knowing not what it wants
except itself: desire—

Thus, do fragments
become logical—

Each page should
be a glass pane
etched with words
not paper, too soft

a field for you
r hand leaving my waist—

"Guantanamo" may pop
up in a poem
but "Guantanamo"
is not just a word—

Read to receive more
than one can return—

*****

: how does one gauge the process of a word's dying?

: this witness so clearly loves his subject. Witnessing love is usually lovely—

: how does one gauge the process of a word's resurrection?

: due to poetic prowess she does justice to her subject—she knows when to get out of the way—

: the matter-of-factness in many poems cannot hide how they are protest poems—

: these poems draw you into a vivid world wrought from turmoil, from trauma, and hold you there with their honesty and empathy—

: *unrelenting*: the consistent difficulty and persistent lyricism combine for an impressive result for which the poet deserves no less than heaven—even if it must be non-paradise: "suffering would be / my salvation"—

: after repulsion I became respectful. It took courage
to act in a way that would lead to apology. It took
a controlled helplessness that served the poems well—

: contemplation, contemplation, contemplation. With Guston. Through Guston. *Beyond Guston.* It never rests inward—contemplation continues forward to what is outside of the poet—

: a book that's more a snapshot, a *still*, rather than a movie. There's no beginning-and-end. The first poem begins with the word "and"—

: the charm of these poems is that even when the poet presents a third-party pronoun, the receptive reader easily transforms it to an "I," thus inhabiting the poem—

: written as if it's an offhand aside, but delivers its message through volcanic impact—

: an encouragement to pay closer attention to what you've already experienced, what you thought you already knew. Poems setting you ablaze, making you look at the world with glowing alien eyes—

: a wonderful *push*-ing by the words as they gallop across the page—

: a home is also a gift. The poet realizes you often receive gifts by first offering gifts—

: that the question arises is welcome for presenting a tiny rip in the book. The rip (reference: wabi sabi) makes the collection more endearing: the reader is not here just to listen to the poems but to engage with them, whether through
    a joust
    square dance
    belly laugh
    thoughtful pause
    or shiver culminating in a deep wince—

: lucidity does not always translate
to freshness in language. But
for poets who've devoted attention to language
                              poems become more radiant—

: space is impossible to depict without non-space—

: requiring poetry to articulate what is invisible—

: as if these poems were written casually
to be minor poems ...
but somehow failed to be minor—

: powerful poems because the poet looked unflinchingly at dark moments and came out of the experience considering herself "Blessed"—

: while many poets use fragments,
the poet's location of unexpected worlds in such fragments
hearkens deep meditation
rather than a skimming of life's vicissitudes—

: It's very difficult to write long hay(na)ku sequences (i.e., more than one tercet) without giving too much weight to merely-connective words like "and", "the" or "a". These pop up in the poet's hay(na)ku but their stress seems equal to the other (usually more significant) words. The result achieves what José García Villa claims about effective poems:
            Each word must be necessary—

: energetically inviting first lines. Like page-turners. Once you've read the first line you're immediately invested—yanked!–into the rest of the poem—

: her caesuras make me think she'd have been right at home in some 7th century
Carolingian monastery—right there with the monks inventing
the period
    the comma
        spaces between words
          and the paragraph return
as ways to insert pauses and end-stops to make text more readable, hence, more
accessible—

: stellar line-breaks turn the read into a rhythm so deeply felt even bones rock and
roll—

: with repetition, parentheticals and other devices, the poet writes
out an energy of unfolding attraction. But the unfolding stutters.
It moves towards, but stutters because falling
in love is not always a smooth, direct path—

: critique does not suffice to create poetry—

: what suffices for poetry? Anything—nothing—all—

: one's ability to withstand pain in a matter where observation and meditation, if
they are to be conducted deeply, are to self-inflict pain—

: love clarifies as much as it clouds vision—

: narrator observes self-as-other—

: I've seen many of these roadside tokens and it is true that the centers of these
fake flower bouquets are usually "too bright"—
        inappropriately so when the matter at hand is grief—

: poems that deliver revelations so keenly they become knives to the gut—

: I don't begrudge this wasting of my time!
It's just too pleasurable!

Like wasting time with the breeze
floating the hammock,
hands behind one's head,
watching the world unfold ...

and occasionally reaching for
a small notebook to jot down some thought
as if the thought will matter
beyond its moment of creation—

: nota bene how the poems are written from a structured starting point instead of
an author's conscious desire to say something specific—

: the poet has trained his eye. That's all a great poet needs sometimes—not an interesting or unusual life, but the ability to see what's not usual in everyday details—

: the *hushed*-ness that surfaces. All these words! And yet. Such quiet!

: how, per James Berger, "language in the proper solution, dissolves, or else reincorporates into unrecognizable, engulfing signals disguised as pieces of the world"—

: the trajectory between the two books: a restless
mind whose vision continues to expand
with all the messiness that such entails—

: that line "he found himself" only to continue in the next line's first word, "adrift," exemplifies meticulous craft—

: her use of double slashes, "/ /," reminds me of cutting—specifically how troubled girls cut their flesh, paradoxically to feel—

: the words—their textures—are ravishing
and *ravished*.

There's a certain flickering light within the poems.
Not bright. Flickering.
Fragile, but one senses one can count on it never dying to dark—

: there's a balancing act. There's balance—

: the poems are quiet. And disquiet—

: if I don't whiff a sense of the mysterious I'm not as moved.
A vase receives but doesn't engage.
As a reader, I'd like to be more than another's vessel—

: wonderful, judicious insertions of "you." As the writing shifts across topics and dimensions, the reader becomes the writer!

: manic jumps between disconnected narrative references to alchemize an organic whole through the body of a poem—

: there's still something to say and/or there's still value in speaking—
despair is not synonymous with giving up—

: there's much wit in these poems, but my favorite manifests love—

: Jazz scaffolds the movements across and between a multiplicity of references to manifest what he quoted from Homer: "We leave home to find ourselves"—

x

: poems contain the paradox of garnets—stones for, say, jewelry but ever evoking blood. Jewels that should be pretty but end up transcending décor—

: I initially thought to use such adjectives as "subversive" and "innovative" (along with more benign but nonetheless sincere terms like "interesting" and "witty"). But I might simply call the poet's point-of-view, thus the poems, to be "open."
                    Open-minded.
                            Open-hearted—

: poems by someone all too aware that no one but "you are the sentry at the watch" of your life. "Only you ... know / [when] you have left your post"—

: to see *the thing as the thing itself* rather than the thing as others say such thing is. I suppose that can be a challenge in the art world—or any other world so invested in cultural capital (Hello, poetry world!)—

: Here, poetry is a metaphor for other forms—a mentor, a college education, religion and/or spirituality (not necessarily the same thing, of course)—that can serve as a saving grace in a life of deprivations while providing a model for transcending victimization—

: why a rant for attachment? Because there's too much *caring* displayed amidst the play. These aren't just text games—

: while the language is straight-forward, the poems avoid the pitfall of projects written for children and "young adults": they do not patronize the targeted young audience, thus, also becoming poems not "too young" for adult readers—

: the total lack of moments that may offer relief, redemption or hope to its critical (pun intended) narrative arc. That's also the collection's strength: its uncompromisingness—the relentlessness of its gaze.

        The eye might not like what it sees but it doesn't flinch—

: such are the vagaries of memory. Gaps are inherent. Loss is inevitable. Fragments are logical—

: I haven't seen you in years. Now, when I read your poems, I think of you as pure light. There is no skin between you and your poems. So though I haven't seen your face, your body, in years, I saw you just seconds ago when I opened your book read from your poem: "At the end of my life I must stagger back to love"—

: apparently, it's a chapbook released to coincide with a poetry reading, as prodded into life by its publisher. Well, I'm glad the publisher got the poet to "get his ass in gear"—

: one of my favorite poetry paradoxes: how reader-response can be most enjoyable when what's read literally does not make sense—

: it would be reductive
to say the poet keeps our attention through an unflagging energy and musicality—
it would be reductive
to posit this poem is based on "all music consist[ing] of mere sounds."

There are too many well-wrought lines that make a reader return for more pondering,
say, "WHEN YOU'RE THE BEST monster"—

: these poems stick in memory. I relish their presence—

: the poems are gorgeous but like beauty behind glass:
    "Don't eavesdrop on the egg"
or
    "Breasts that hatch / Like music"
Each page should be a glass pane etched with text. Paper seems too soft (a field) for these words—

: the poems result from a two-poet collaboration, but no individual author stands out
except for Author #3, that presence that is more than the sum of "1 + 1"—

: this transition phase between two worlds, two cultures, two languages through which a concept like "affection or / disease" makes sense though they are not literal opposites: "Let me land in the open air"—

: self-deprecation is popular for its effectiveness. It draws a reader in through empathy if not sympathy. It draws the reader in through shared amusement. It draws the reader in through an admiration of wit. It even allows one to get away with bombast. To wit, there's a reason why many poets—and I implicate myself—lapse to self-deprecation.   But I hadn't realized how much I'd gotten tired of it, until I read this taut, intelligent collection wherein I found the antidote. This poet has written justifiably confident poems—

: a criticism that doesn't dampen appreciation—indeed, it heightens appreciation for offering additional information about process without making impossible a direct engagement with the result—

: poems like "food wine," relying on its context versus its self—

: there's a passion in this endeavor far transcending the placement of a poem in a journal in order to get credit and/or further a career. Here, I'm not intending to criticize careerism in the arts so much as acknowledging the many ways through which a poem or art can find a "home" without needing the nod of an establishment—

: "knowing-through-feeling" is the indigenized equivalent of (Western) phenomenology, according to Katrina de Guia and is critical for what Leny M. Strobel calls "re-indigenization." Decolonization is relevant

for if one is to discover indigenous values, one must heal
from the effects of colonialism, the force that supplanted
indigeneity with modernity—

: poets have performed their art devoid of clothes. But revealing details about finances and health is more exposure than unclothing flesh. Skin still covers. This poet shows that the definition of "disclosure" is not just to show one's ass but to show it in all of its cellulite- or acne- as well as diseased-without-health-care-ridden glory. This poet has earned to right to proclaim: KISS MY ASS—

: ENDGAMES is the purr-fect title for this collection that delivers an ACE

of a serve to poetry's attempts to write itself. I call the works (tennis-related) Aces since each delivers a sense of completely having said it all (whatever that it is). There's no need for the reader to dither as to what the work signifies or where it's going (much as one goes back and forth in tennis). Each work delivers its world complete, and one's job as a reader/viewer is not to "complete" it with one's subjective response (as is encouraged by some deliberately open-ended poem) but just

to witness it … and marvel—

: a radiance so matured even darkness becomes luminous—

: the poems as ghosts of what they may have hoped to become—

: definitional mysteries—

: the facts about which poems are made—"Guantanamo"
may pop up in one poem but "Guantanamo" is not just a word—

: she doesn't look at the box
that features the image
she's trying to recreate
from numerous puzzle pieces,

feeling she'll be more transported
by the result if she doesn't know
what awaited her piecing-together-fingers—

: enchanting—

: a poet who gives more than we ever could return—

It moves towards but stutters like love's rarely smooth path—

Observation and meditation, if conducted deeply, are to self-inflict pain—

Fake flowers are often too bright, inappropriately so when the matter at hand is grief—

A restless mind whose vision expands, unafraid of mess—

Their words—texture—are ravishing and ravished—

The poems are quiet. And disquiet—

To see the thing as the thing itself—

An orphan's rant for attachment—

Fragments are logical—

Each page should be a glass pane etched with words. Paper seems too soft a field—

"Guantanamo" may pop up in a poem but "Guantanamo" is not just a word—

To receive more than one can return—

ON PROCESS: ANOTHER WAY TO SCULPT

To create this poem, I first reviewed 86 publications by poets. Reviews were chosen at random from the poet's inventory of poetry reviews. The poem began (but continued beyond) excerpts from the reviews annotated in the order listed below. All of the reviews (except for one because I deemed it "negative" and I usually—though not always—prefer not to write negatively on poetry) were first published in *Galatea Resurrects (A Poetry Engagement)*. Reviews were conducted on:

Obsolete—an alphabet of poems inspired by dead words by Katie Haegele, with design by Noah Beytin (self-published, Jenkintown, PA, 2008)

Brushstrokes and glances by Djelloul Marbrook (Dearbrook Editions, Cumberland, ME, 2010)

Had Slaves by Catherine Sasanov (Firewheel Editions, Danbury, CT, 2010)

info ration by Stan Apps (Make Now, Los Angeles, 2007)

RED WALLS by James Tolan (Dos Madres Press, Loveland, OH, 2011)

My Life as a Doll by Elizabeth Kirschner (Autumn House Press, Pittsburgh, PA, 2008)

TO BE HUMAN IS TO BE A CONVERSATION by Andrea Rexilius (Rescue + Press, Milwaukee, WI, 2011)

There Are People Who Think That Painters Shouldn't Talk: A GUSTONBOOK by Patrick James Dunagan (The Post-Apollo Press, Sausalito, CA, 2011)

STILL: OF THE EARTH AS THE ARK WHICH DOES NOT MOVE by Matthew Cooperman (Counterpath Press, Denver, 2011)

Radiator by NF Huth (Laughing/Ouch/Cube/Publications / Leafe Press, Nottingham, U.K. and Claremont, CA, 2011)

Blue Collar Poet by G. Emil Reutter (StoneGarden.net Publishing, Danville, CA, 2009)

WAIFS AND STRAYS by Micah Ballard (City Lights, San Francisco, 2011)

DRAFT 96: VELOCITY by Rachel Blau DuPlessis (little red leaves textile editions, http://www.textileseries.com/, 2011)

we / cum ::: come / in the yield fields / amongst statues with interior arms by j/j hastain (above / ground press, Ottawa, 2012)

asymptotic lover//thermodynamic vents by j/j hastain (BlazeVOX Books, Buffalo, New York, 2008)

ENGINE EMPIRE by Cathy Park Hong (W.W. Norton and Company, New York / London, 2012)

CHINOISERIE by Karen Rigby (Ahsahta Press, Boise, ID, 2012)

HAVE by Marc Gaba (Tupelo Press, North Adams, MA, 2011)

catch light by Sarah O'Brien (Coffee House Press, Minneapolis, Minn., 2009)

Bending at the Elbow by Matyei Yankelevich (Minutes BOOKS, Hadley, MA, 2011)

ARDOR: poems of life by Janine Canan (Pilgrims Publishing, Varanasi, India, 2012)

Common Time by Chris Pusateri (Steerage Press, Boulder, CO & Normal, IL, 2012)

Angles of Incidents by Jon Curley (Dos Madres Press Inc., Loveland, OH, 2012)

cloudfang :: cakedirt by Daniela Olszewska (Horse Less Press, Providence, RI, 2012)

The Collected Poems of Lucille Clifton 1965-2010, Edited by Kevin Young and Michael S. Glaser (BOA Editions, Rochester, N.Y., 2012)

MAY APPLE DEEP by Michael Sikkema (Horse Less Press, Providence, RI, 2012)

The Romances and other poems by Micah Cavaleri (Dead Man Publishing, Dollar Bay, Michigan, 2012)

clarity and other poems by Thomas Fink (Marsh Hawk Press, New York, 2008)

MERIDIAN by Kathleen Jesme (Tupelo Press, North Adams, MA, 2012)

WORK IS LOVE MADE VISIBLE: Poetry and Family Photographs by Jeanetta Calhoun Mish (West End Press, Albuquerque, NM, 2009)

THE BODY DOUBLE: a long poem by Jared Harel (Brooklyn Arts Press, Brooklyn, 2012)

Waxwings by Daniel Nathan Terry (Lethe Press, Maple Shade, N.J., 2012)

ONE BIRD FALLING by CB Follett (Time Being Books, St. Louis, Missouri, 2011)

AT THE TURNING OF THE LIGHT by CB Follett (Salmon Run Press, Chugiak, AK, 2001)

VISIBLE BONES by CB Follett (Plain View Press, Austin, 1998)

ITEMS by Tom Jenks (if p then q, Manchester, U.K., 2013)

Memory Cards by Susan Schultz (Singing Horse Press, San Diego, CA 2011)

THE GRAPEVINE by Richard Lopez (24th street irregular press, Sacramento, CA 2003)

All This Falling Away by Tim Armentrout (Dusi/e, Switzerland, 2007)

PRIOR by James Berger (BlazeVOX Books, Buffalo, N.Y., 2013)

modulations by Márton Koppány (Otoliths, Rockhampton, Australia, 2010)

Addenda by Márton Koppány (Otoliths, Rockhampton, Australia, 2012)

THE READER by Márton Koppány (Runaway Spoon Press, Port Charlotte, FL, 2011)

Rounding the Human Corners by Linda Hogan (Coffee House Press, Minneapolis, 2008)

Renegade // Heart by Lisa M. Cole (Blood Pudding Press, 2013)

He Looked Beyond My Faults and Saw My Needs by Leonard Gontarek (Hanging Loose Press, Brooklyn, N.Y., 2013)

Deja Vu Diner by Leonard Gontarek (Autumn House Press, Pittsburgh, PA 2006)

door of thin skins by Shira Dentz (CavanKerry Press, Fort Lee, New Jersey, 2013)

And so for you there is no heartbreak by K. Lorraine Graham (Dusie chaps, a kollektiv, Switzerland, 2007)

Psychedelic Norway by John Colburn (Coffee House Press, Minneapolis, Minn., 2013)

The Unfinished: Books I-VI by Mark DuCharme (BlazeVOX Books, Buffalo, N.Y., 2013)

*BIG BAD ASTERISK** by Carlo Matos (BlazeVOX [books], Buffalo, N.Y., 2013)

New Orleans Variations and Paris Ouroboros by Paul Pines (Dos Madres, Loveland, OH, 2013)

Sister, Blood and Bone by Paula Cary (Blood Pudding Press, Ohio, 2013)

pleth by j/j hastain and Marthe Reed (Unlikely Books, Lafayette, LA, 2013)

from behind the blind by Robert Murphy (Dos Madres Press, Loveland, OH, 2013)

A Thing Among Things: The Art of Jasper Johns by John Yau (Distributed Arts Publishers, New York, 2008)

A Place to Stand by Jimmy Santiago Baca (Grove Press, New York, 2001)

Behave: California Rant 66 by Steve Tills (dPress, Sebastopol, CA, 2004)

Behind the Wheel: Poems About Driving by Janet S. Wong (Margaret K. Elderberry Books/ Simon & Schuster, New York, 1999)

Cleaving by Dion Farquhar (Poets Corner Press, Stockton, CA, 2007)

Zamboanguena by Corrine Fitzpatrick (Sona Books, Brooklyn, 2007)

Amigo Warfare by Eric Gamalinda (Cherry Grove Editions, Cincinnati, OH, 2007)

Lyrics From A Dead Language by Eric Gamalinda (Anvil Publishing, Manila,1991)

nineteen hours (radio edit) by Jim Wagner (chapbookpublisher.com, Pennsylvania, 2009)

100 Scenes by Tim Gaze (Transgressor / Wider Screenings, 2010)

A Musics by Carrie Hunter (arrow as arrow, 2010)

Open Night by Aaron Lowinger (Transmission Press, San Francisco, 2008)

TIME OF SKY / CASTLES IN THE AIR by Ayane Kawata, Translated by Sawako Nakayasu (Litmus Press, Brooklyn, 2010)

EASY EDEN by Micah Ballard and James Patrick Dunagan (PUSH, San Francisco, 2009)

Analfabeto / An Alphabet by Ellen Baxt (Shearsman Books, Exeter, U.K., 2007)

I Was the Jukebox by Sandra Beasley (W.W. Norton & Co., New York, 2010)

For the Ordinary Artist: Short Reviews, Occasional Pieces & More by Bill Berkson (BlazeVOX Books, Buffalo, N.Y., 2010)

Portrait and Dream: New and Selected Poems by Bill Berkson (Coffee House Press, Minneapolis, 2009)

BALLISTICS by Billy Collins (Random House, New York, 2008)

BONE BOUQUET: a journal of poetry by women, Vol. 1, Issue 1, Winter 2011 (no locale cited, 2011)

INSIDES SHE SWALLOWED by Sasha Pimentel Chacon (West End Press, Albuquerque, NM, 2010)

EASTER SUNDAY by Barbara Jane Reyes (ypolita press, San Francisco, 2008)

Simon J. Ortiz: A Poetic Legacy of Indigenous Continuance, Edited by Susan Berry Brill de Ramirez and Evelina Zuni Lucero (University of New Mexico Press, Albuquerque, NM, 2009)

DISCLOSURE by Dana Teen Lomax (Dusie Kollektiv, 2009)

ENDGAMES by Márton Koppány (Otoliths, Rockhampton, Australia, 2008)

AS IF IT FELL FROM THE SUN: An Etherdome Anthology: Ten Years of Women's Writing, Edited by Colleen Lookingbill & Elizabeth Robinson (Includes Merle Bachman, Faith Barrett, Margaret Butterfield, Erica Carpenter, Valerie Coulton, Caroline Crumpacker, Susanne Dyckman, Kelly Everding, Renata Ewing, Amanda Field, Kate Greenstreet, Anne Heide, Brydie MPherson Kuchi, Erica Lewis, Susan Manchester, Linda Norton, Roberta Olson, Megan Pruiett, Lisa Rappoport, Sarah Suzor, and Stacy Szymaszek) (EtherDome Chapbooks/Instance, San Francisco & Boulder, 2012)

Apparition Poems by Adam Fieled (BlazeVOX Books, Buffalo, N.Y., 2010)

Forget Reading by Anthony Hawley (Shearsman Books, Exeter, U.K., 2008)

Genji Monogatari by Mark Young (Otoliths, Rockhampton, Australia, 2010)

HOUSES: a poem by CB Follett (Tebot Bach, Huntington Beach, CA, 2011)

ntst: the collected pwoermds of Geof Huth (if p then q, Manchester, U.K., 2010)

NO GENDER: REFLECTIONS ON THE LIFE & WORK OF kari edwards, Edited by Julian Brolaski, erica kaufman & E. Tracy Grinnell (Includes Cara Benson, Frances Blau, Mark Brasuell, Julian T. Brolaski, Reed Bye, Marcus Civin, CAConrad, Donna de la Perrière, E. Tracy Grinnell, Rob Halpern, Jen Hofer, Brenda Iijima, Lisa Jarnot, erica kaufman, Kevin Killian, Wendy Kramer, Joseph Lease, Rachel Levitsky, Joan MacDonald, Bill Marsh, Chris Martin, Yedda Morrison, Eileen Myles, Akilah Oliver, Tim Peterson, Ellen Redbird, Leslie Scalapino, Michael Smoler, Sherman Souther, Eleni Stecopoulos, and Anne Waldman) (a Venn Diagram Production by Litmus Press / Belladonna Books, Brooklyn, New York, 2009)

SELECTED NOTES TO POEMS

(ABANDONING MISERY
A "datsan" is a Buddhist colony; the poem partly refers to a trip to the Igolvinsk datsan in Siberia in April 1996.

(JANUARY
The poem's ending was inspired by my beloved son Michael's vocabulary-expanding lessons in preparation for taking his SAT tests.

(THE CONTROLLING AGENT
The first and last line of the poem come from an untitled poem for, and written during correspondence with, Tom Beckett:

> The present is thin
>
> as thin as action
> when action's completion
> transforms present
> to past
>
> Thin for the act
> can occur (thus
> be completed) in phases
> which can be so thin
> they are invisible
>
> but still exist
>
> So thin it might
> feel imagined
>
> The thinness of
> the present—
> another reason
> to treasure
>
> or fear
>
> in any event, respect
>
> the past
>
>   *
>
> The past is thick

(THE INVESTMENT BANKER
The poem is rooted in a Sept. 13, 1996 reading by Mei-mei Berssenbrugge at

the Asian American Writers Workshop which was attended by friends who were investment bankers from Union Bank of Switzerland, Merrill Lynch and Morgan Stanley.

HEART POETRY: A CRITIQUE

Certain poems and poets are quoted from reviews written on the referenced books:
—"suffering would be / my salvation" is from "My Life As A Doll" by Elizabeth Kirschner
—"language in the proper solution, dissolves, or else reincorporates into unrecognizable, engulfing signals disguised as pieces of the world" is from James Berger's bio in his book PRIOR.
—"he found himself / adrift" is from "Alone" by Linda Hogan
—"you are the sentry at the watch [of your life" and "[O]nly you ... knows / [when] you alone have left your post" are from "Who Goes There" by Robert Murphy
—"the thing as the thing itself" is from *A Thing Among Things: The Art of Jasper Johns* by John Yau
—"At the end of my life I must stagger back to love" is from "DMZ" by Eric Gamalinda
—"WHEN YOU'RE THE BEST monster" is from "A Musics" by Carrie Hunter
—"Breasts that hatch / Like music" is from "Time of the Sky" by Ayane Kawata, Translated by Sawako Nakayasu
—"affection or / disease" and "Let me land in the open air" are from *Analfabeto / An Alphabet* by Ellen Baxt

ACKNOWLEDGEMENTS

Everlasting gratitude to Marsh Hawk Press and especially my in-house editor Thomas Fink and managing editor Sandy McIntosh. Thanks as well to Michelle Bautista for constant loving support as well as design and technical expertise for not just my books but my life! A salute to the Gotan Project and JS Bach for music during the editing process. I'm also indebted to the following publications and editors for first publishing, or accepting for future publication, individual poems (some in earlier versions) as follows:

Cerise Press, 2013, Editors Sally Molini, Karen Rigby, Fiona Sze-Lorrain
DUSIE, 2014, Editor Susanna Gardner and Guest Editor Carrie Hunter
eccolinguistics 2.1, 2013, Editor Jared Schickling
HOUSE ORGAN, Editor Kenneth Warren
Marsh Hawk Press Review, 2012, Guest Editor Norman Finkelstein
Marsh Hawk Review, Spring 2014, Guest Editor Mary Mackey
Moria Poetry, Editor William Allegrezza
Moss Trill, Editor William Allegrezza
Muddy River Poetry Review, 2012, Editor Zvi A. Sesling
{m}aganda magazine, 2013, Literary Editor Joan Victoria Tionko
{m}aganda magazine, 2014, Literary Editor Nicole Arca
On Barcelona, Editor Halvard Johnson
Perihelion: A Journal of Poetry—"End of Empire," Editors Dion Farquhar and James Maughn, Editor-at-large: Jean Vengua
Poets & Artists, 2013, Editor Didi Menendez
Talisman, Editors Ed Foster and Lisa Bourbeau
Otoliths, Editor Mark Young
Van Gogh's Ear, Editor Ian Ayres
Yellow Field, 2012, Editor Edric Mesmer

"(ADULTERY" was recorded with an alternate title, "(ANGLE," for *OurOwnVoice*, Editors Reme Grefalda and Aileen Ibardaloza

"(INSOMNIA'S LULLABYE" will be featured in the forthcoming book, *Mandirigmang Babae: a Kali Journey of a Woman Warrior,* by Michelle Bautista

The essay "EMMY CATEDRAL'S INVITATION TO HER 'DANCES IN THE DARK'" first appeared in *OurOwnVoice*, June 2005, Editors Reme Grefalda and Aileen Ibardaloza (for more illustrations, go to http://www.oovrag.com/essays/essay2005c-6.shtml)

ABOUT THE AUTHOR

Eileen R. Tabios loves books, and has released more than 20 print, five electronic and 1 CD poetry collections; an art essay collection; a "collected novels" book; a poetry essay/interview anthology; a short story collection; and an experimental biography. She has also exhibited visual art and visual poetry in the United States and Asia. Recipient of the Philippines' National Book Award for Poetry for her first poetry collection, she has crafted an award-winning body of work that is unique for melding ekphrasis with transcolonialism. Her poems have been translated into Spanish, Italian, Tagalog, Japanese, Portuguese, Polish, Greek, computer-generated hybrid languages, Paintings, Video, Drawings, Visual Poetry, Mixed Media Collages, Kali Martial Arts, Music, Modern Dance and Sculpture. She invented the poetic form "hay(na)ku" which has been used by poets around the world, and is author of the first book-length haybun (a hay(na)ku derivation), *147 MILLION ORPHANS*. She also has edited, co-edited or conceptualized ten anthologies of poetry, fiction and essays in addition to serving as editor or guest editor for various literary journals. She maintains a biblioliphic blog, "Eileen Verbs Books"; edits *Galatea Resurrects,* a popular poetry review; steers the literary and arts publisher Meritage Press; serves as Library Director for *BIBLIOTHECA INVISIBILIS* (an online library that archives conceptualizations of the invisible), and frequently curates thematic online poetry projects including *LinkedIn Poetry Recommendations* (a recommended list of contemporary poetry books).

TITLES FROM MARSH HAWK PRESS

Jane Augustine, *A Woman's Guide to Mountain Climbing, Night Lights, Arbor Vitae*
Tom Beckett, ~~*Dipstick*~~*/(Diptych)*
Sigman Byrd, *Under the Wanderer's Star*
Patricia Carlin, *Quantum Jitters, Original Green*
Claudia Carlson, *Pocket Park, The Elephant House*
Meredith Cole, *Miniatures*
Neil de la Flor, *An Elephant's Memory of Blizzards, Almost Dorothy*
Chard deNiord, *Sharp Golden Thorn*
Sharon Dolin, *Serious Pink*
Steve Fellner, *The Weary World Rejoices, Blind Date with Cavafy*
Thomas Fink, *Joyride, Peace Conference, Clarity and Other Poems, After Taxes, Gossip: A Book of Poems*
Norman Finkelstein, *Inside the Ghost Factory, Passing Over*
Edward Foster, *Dire Straits, The Beginning of Sorrows, What He Ought To Know, Mahrem: Things Men Should Do for Men*
Paolo Javier, *The Feeling Is Actual*
Burt Kimmelman, *Somehow*
Burt Kimmelman and Fred Caruso, *The Pond at Cape May Point*
Basil King, *77 Beasts: Basil King's Bestiary, Mirage*
Martha King, *Imperfect Fit*
Phillip Lopate, *At the End of the Day: Selected Poems and An Introductory Essay*
Mary Mackey, *Travelers With No Ticket Home, Sugar Zone, Breaking the Fever*
Jason McCall, *Dear Hero,*
Sandy McIntosh, *Cemetery Chess: Selected and New Poems, Ernesta, in the Style of the Flamenco, Forty-Nine Guaranteed Ways to Escape Death, The After-Death History of My Mother, Between Earth and Sky*
Stephen Paul Miller, *There's Only One God and You're Not It, Fort Dad, The Bee Flies in May, Skinny Eighth Avenue*
Daniel Morris, *If Not for the Courage, Bryce Passage*
Sharon Olinka, *The Good City*
Justin Petropoulos, *Eminent Domain*
Paul Pines, *Last Call at the Tin Palace, Divine Madness*
Jacquelyn Pope, *Watermark*
Karin Randolph, *Either She Was*
Rochelle Ratner, *Ben Casey Days, Balancing Acts, House and Home*
Michael Rerick, *In Ways Impossible to Fold*
Corrine Robins, *Facing It: New and Selected Poems, Today's Menu, One Thousand Years*
Eileen R. Tabios, *SUN STIGMATA (Sculpture Poems); The Thorn Rosary: Selected Prose Poems and New (1998–2010); The Light Sang As It Left Your Eyes: Our Autobiography; I Take Thee, English, for My Beloved; Reproductions of the Empty Flagpole*
Eileen R. Tabios and j/j hastain, *the relational elations of ORPHANED ALGEBRA*
Susan Terris, *Ghost of Yesterday, Natural Defenses*
Madeline Tiger, *Birds of Sorrow and Joy*
Harriet Zinnes, *New and Selected Poems, Weather Is Whether, Light Light or the Curvature of the Earth, Whither Nonstopping, Drawing on the Wall*